INFLUENCER MARKETING TRENDS

LEVERAGING SOCIAL MEDIA INFLUENCERS FOR BRAND PROMOTION

Beyond Design Fashion Product Development's Joint Impacts Tested Methods for Beating Competition, Utilizing Current Viral Trends, Creating Massive Brand on Social media's

RICHARD N. WILLIAMS

TABLE OF CONTENTS

INTRODUCTI ON

TO INFLUENCER MARKETING

In the speedy universe of promoting, one idea has arisen to reshape the manner in which we associate with crowds: Force to be reckoned with Showcasing. This isn't a story of a far off past, yet a cutting edge account that has previously changed endless organizations and people into examples of overcoming adversity.

Meet Joyce, a growing business person with an imaginative vision and a strong soul. She had sent off a little internet based shop selling high quality gems, however the underlying excursion was testing. Battling to acquire perceivability in the packed web based business market, Joyce understood that she really wanted a new methodology. Also, that is the point at which she found the distinct advantage: Powerhouse Advertising.

Joyce wasn't beginning without any preparation. She had seen forces to be reckoned with advancing items, however she didn't completely grasp the potential until she dug further. She drenches herself in the realm of force to be reckoned with promoting, concentrating on its complexities and gaining from specialists. Her devotion to understanding this new idea was the most vital phase in her motivating process.

In any case, training alone wasn't sufficient. To carry out her newly discovered information, Joyce required the right powerhouse to work with. She directed careful exploration, planning to find somebody whose values lined up with her image. That is the point at which she coincidentally found Emma, a design powerhouse known for her realness and obligation to feasible items.

With an open heart and a thoroughly examined pitch, Joyce contacted Emma. The reaction she got was a thumbs up as well as a common vision. Emma was eager to team up on a venture that mixed her enthusiasm for manageability with Joyce's eco-accommodating gems. It was an organization produced on shared values, and moving others was predetermined.

Their cooperation was going to unfurl into something phenomenal. Emma, with her certified association with her crowd, made true happy exhibiting Joyce's gems. She went past customary publicizing and shared her own account of how these frill had turned into a significant piece of her life. This reverberated with her supporters, who embraced the brand, not as an item but rather as a way of life.

The effect was quick. Joyce's web-based shop encountered a flood in orders. What started as an unobtrusive business was presently encountering dramatic development. Be that as it may, Joyce wasn't happy with simply this underlying achievement. She comprehended the need to adjust and scale her powerhouse promoting procedure.

Along with Emma, they conceptualized imaginative plans to draw in their crowd on a more profound level. They sent off a challenge empowering clients to share their own accounts associated with the gems. The reaction was overpowering. Individuals spilled their guts, representing how these hand tailored pieces had become more than adornments; they were images of solidarity, strength, and individual change.

These contacting stories enhanced the brand as well as made a real feeling of the local area. Emma, as the essence of the brand, kept on being the extension between Joyce's manifestations and the hearts of her crowd. Their organization had developed into a genuine joint effort, where legitimacy and shared values stayed at the center.

The outcome of Joyce's store was not just about benefit; it was a demonstration of development, versatility, and the force of powerhouse promoting. The genuine change lay in the tales of individuals who had tracked down trust and motivation in the excursion of a little gems business.

As their image developed, so did their effect. Joyce's eco-accommodating methodology reached out to bundling, and the pair started magnanimous coordinated efforts, making items where a level of the returns went towards causes the two of them had faith in. Their story turned into a wellspring of motivation, demonstrating the way that business achievement could exist together with sure friendly change.

In this motivating story, we witness the change of Joyce, who once confronted vulnerability, into an effective business visionary with a devoted local area of clients. We perceive how Emma, with her certified soul, turned into an impetus for this change, utilizing her leverage to rouse, interface, and make enduring change. Together, they displayed the force of powerhouse promoting to rouse and enhance, showing that achievement remains inseparable with a certified association with the crowd.

In the realm of powerhouse promoting, Joyce and Emma's story is only one of numerous instances of how this creative methodology can possibly achieve a significant change in business and then some. It's a demonstration of the possibility that, in the computerized age, the associations we make can be pretty much as significant as the items we sell. Furthermore, it's an update that earnestly, receptiveness, and a tough soul, anybody can transform their vision into a reality, moving and changing lives en route.

What Is Influencer Marketing?

The Force of Advanced Influence

In the always developing scene of promoting, one procedure that has acquired huge noticeable quality as of late is forced to be reckoned with advertising. This inventive methodology exploits the web-based entertainment age, where people who have fabricated significant internet based followings can use impressive impact over their crowd's viewpoints and buying choices. In this 800-word investigation, we'll dive into the central ideas of powerhouse promoting, its advancement, and its effect on the universe of publicizing.

Characterizing Powerhouse Promoting

At its center, powerhouse promoting is a type of online entertainment showcasing the impact and reach of people who have laid out believability in a particular industry or specialty. These people, known as powerhouses, can go from big names to specialists, devotees, or even miniature forces to be reckoned with. What separates powerhouses is their capacity to draw in and interface with their crowd on an individual level, making them a fundamental part of contemporary showcasing procedures.

Powerhouse advertising works by cooperating with these forces to be reckoned with to advance items, administrations, or brands to their devotees. Rather than depending entirely on customary publicizing techniques, brands tap into a powerhouse's genuineness and dependability to contact a more open crowd.

The Development of Powerhouse Promoting

While powerhouse promotion may appear to be a new peculiarity, its foundations follow back to superstar supporters, which have been a piece of publicizing for quite a long time. The significant shift happened with the ascent of online entertainment stages, especially Instagram and YouTube, in the mid 2010s. These stages gave a phase to individuals to impart their lives and skill to a worldwide crowd.

In this new scene, powerhouses arose naturally. They acquired gigantic followings by delivering appealing substance, sharing their encounters, and offering skill in different specialties, from magnificence and design to wellness, travel, and then some. Their supporters, frequently numbering in large numbers, trust their viewpoints and proposals.

Advertisers before long perceived the capability of powerhouse organizations, and force to be reckoned with showcasing as far as we might be concerned today started to come to fruition. Brands started teaming up with powerhouses to make valid substances that exhibited their items or administrations. This approach felt more certified than conventional commercials and reverberated with crowds.

The Effect of Powerhouse Promoting

Powerhouse showcasing has made a permanent imprint on the promoting scene in light of multiple factors:

Trust and Validness: Forces to be reckoned with have assembled their crowds on trust and realness. Their adherents view them as companions instead of corporate elements, making their support more solid.

Designated Reach: Powerhouses frequently have explicit specialties or socioeconomics they take care of. This permits brands to contact a profoundly designated crowd that is as of now inspired by their items or administrations.

Engagement: Powerhouse made content will in general produce more significant levels of commitment than customary publicizing. Their presents frequently lead to additional preferences, remarks, and offers.

Content Creation: Forces to be reckoned with are content makers by their own doing. Cooperating with them can give a constant flow of imagination and drawing happiness that can be reused for promotion.

Quantifiable Outcomes: In contrast to some conventional showcasing strategies, powerhouse advertising can give quantifiable outcomes. Measurements like preferences, remarks, offers, and connection snaps can be followed to evaluate crusade adequacy.

Worldwide Reach: The compass of powerhouses stretches out across borders, making powerhouse showcasing a worldwide system for brands hoping to extend their client base.

Sorts of Powerhouses

Forces to be reckoned with come in different sizes and specializations, taking care of a large number of enterprises and socioeconomics. Here are a few normal sorts of powerhouses:

Celebrities: These are notable figures, frequently from media outlets, who have an expansive and different following.

Macro-Influencers: With followings going from 100,000 to a few million, full scale powerhouses are specialists or devotees in their particular specialties.

Micro-Influencers: Miniature powerhouses have more modest followings, commonly in the scope of

1,000 to 100,000, yet they are exceptionally particular and can significantly affect specialty markets.

Nano-Influencers: Nano-powerhouses have the littlest followings, generally under 1,000, however their impact can be strong inside very close networks.

Brand Diplomats: Some powerhouses lay out continuous associations with brands, becoming brand envoys who reliably advance a particular organization's items or administrations.

Challenges and Moral Contemplations

Notwithstanding its many benefits, force to be reckoned with promoting likewise faces difficulties and moral contemplations. These incorporate issues connected with validness, straightforwardness, and the potential for powerhouse burnout. As powerhouse advertising keeps on advancing, so do the guidelines and rules administering the training, pointed toward guaranteeing decency and straightforwardness for both forces to be reckoned with and their crowds.

All in all, powerhouse showcasing addresses a huge change in the realm of publicizing. It tackles the impact and reach of people who have acquired the trust of their internet based networks to advance items and administrations. As the computerized scene keeps on developing, force to be reckoned with promoting is ready to stay a strong power in the showcasing systems of brands around the world, stressing the force of genuine, engaging substance and human associations in the computerized age.

The Power of Social Media Influencers

Virtual entertainment has changed the manner in which we impart, associate, and consume data. Perhaps the main improvement inside the domain of virtual entertainment is the development of powerhouses. These people have outfitted the force of stages like Instagram, YouTube, TikTok, and Twitter to hoard enormous and drew in followings. They employ colossal impact, affecting patterns, brands, and customer conduct. The force of online entertainment powerhouses is obvious, and it's changing the elements of promoting and correspondence in significant ways.

Forces to be reckoned with as Innovators

In the time of web-based entertainment, patterns travel every which way at a remarkable speed. Powerhouses, frequently early adopters themselves, assume an urgent part in molding these patterns. Whether it's style, excellence, wellness, or way of life decisions, powerhouses set up for what's stylish. Their genuineness and appeal resound with their supporters, making their support profoundly enticing. Brands perceive the capacity of powerhouses to begin, sustain, and enhance patterns, and they look to team up with them to remain applicable in the consistently advancing buyer scene.

Validness and Appeal

One of the principal motivations behind why virtual entertainment powerhouses are so strong is their capacity to interface with their crowd on an individual level. Not at all like conventional VIPs, forces to be reckoned with are viewed as congenial and appealing. Their devotees see them as certified and genuine, which encourages a feeling of trust. This validness makes powerhouse advertising staggeringly viable, as it takes advantage of the natural human longing for certifiable, dependable suggestions.

Arriving at Specialty Crowds

Web-based entertainment forces to be reckoned with are not one-size-fits-all. There are powerhouses for each specialty and interest. From foodies to gamers, from eco-cognizant supporters to pet sweethearts, there's a powerhouse for each taste. This degree of specialization permits brands to target explicit socioeconomics with accuracy. For example, a beauty care products organization can team up with a marvel powerhouse who has some expertise in skincare and cosmetics instructional exercises to contact an exceptionally drawn in and significant crowd. The capacity to arrive at specialty crowds is a demonstration of the flexibility and force of virtual entertainment powerhouses in showcasing.

Unfiltered Content and Straightforwardness

Virtual entertainment powerhouses frequently give unfiltered and crude substance, which diverges from the cleaned and arranged pictures of conventional promotion. This straightforwardness reverberates with crowds looking for credibility. Numerous powerhouses share their own accounts, difficulties, and weaknesses, cultivating a feeling of association with their supporters. Their receptiveness and eagerness to share both the ups and downs of life make them more appealing and reliable, further improving their impact.

Influence on Shopper Conduct

Forces to be reckoned with have the ability to shape shopper conduct in significant ways. Their item supports, audits, and suggestions hold critical weight. At the point when powerhouses advance an item, their supporters are bound to think about buying it. This impact is obvious in the ascent of subsidiary showcasing and the utilization of special codes exceptional to each powerhouse. Brands track the outcome of these codes and prize powerhouses appropriately, exhibiting the immediate connection between force to be reckoned with proposals and shopper activities.

Social and Natural Effect

The force of web-based entertainment powerhouses reaches out past showcasing and item supports. Numerous powerhouses utilize their foundation to advocate for social and natural causes. They can focus on major problems, prepare their adherents for altruistic undertakings, and even impact popular assessment. For example, environmental change activists like Greta Thunberg have bridged online entertainment to bring issues to light about natural issues and move worldwide activity. This features the potential for powerhouses to drive positive change and add to social and natural causes.

Difficulties and Discussions

While the impact of web-based entertainment powerhouses is certain, it isn't without its difficulties and contentions. One of the essential worries is credibility. Some powerhouses have confronted analysis for advancing items or ways of life that they don't really support. This can disintegrate trust and realness, which are the foundations of their impact. Accordingly, numerous forces to be reckoned with are currently more straightforward about supported content and organizations, and some have taken on a strategy of just advancing items they really use and put stock in.

Another test is the potential for deception or hurtful counsel. To whom much is given, much will be expected, and forces to be reckoned with should be mindful about the data they scatter. Some have confronted reactions for sharing pseudoscientific cases or wellbeing exhortations without legitimate capabilities. To resolve these issues, stages and administrative bodies have executed rules, yet the obligation eventually rests with the powerhouses to guarantee they are giving precise and safe substance.

The force of virtual entertainment powerhouses is an amazing powerhouse in the cutting edge computerized scene. Their capacity to shape patterns, impact customer conduct, and associate with specialty crowds is reshaping promoting and correspondence systems. The genuineness, appeal, and straightforwardness they bring to their substance make them profoundly enticing to their devotees. While difficulties and contentions exist, the potential for positive effect on friendly and natural issues is apparent. As virtual entertainment keeps on developing, the force of powerhouses is probably going to stay a prevailing and groundbreaking power in the web-based world.

The Evolution of Influencer Marketi

As of late, powerhouse showcasing has arisen as a predominant power in the realm of publicizing and advancement. This strong technique, which uses people with a huge web based following to embrace items and administrations, has turned into a critical part of many organizations' promoting plans.

The idea of powerhouses isn't altogether new. Superstars and specialists have for some time been tapped to advance items and administrations. Notwithstanding, what recognizes the advancement of powerhouse promoting is the democratization of impact. It's not just about Elite famous people any longer; it's about anybody with a significant following, frequently in specialty networks, who can apply an extensive effect.

In the beginning of the web, force to be reckoned with showcasing was a long way from being a standard idea. The web was still in its early stages, and virtual entertainment as far as we might be concerned today didn't exist. Notwithstanding, a forerunner to powerhouse promoting was at that point in progress with bloggers and early web gatherings. These people shared their contemplations, conclusions, and proposals, collecting supporters who confided in their skill. This trust laid the preparation for the powerhouse advertising upheaval.

The ascent of web-based entertainment stages, like Facebook, Twitter, and Instagram, gave powerhouses the devices they expected to reach and draw in with a worldwide crowd. The stages permitted people to accumulate supporters who respected their ways of life, design decisions, or aptitude. Brands started to perceive the expectations in these web-based characters and started to shape organizations with them.

The beginning of powerhouse promotion saw an emphasis on full scale powerhouses - those with many thousands or even large numbers of supporters. Brands were attracted to their huge reach and the commitment of wide openness. In any case, as the business developed, so did the techniques.

Miniature powerhouses, with more modest yet exceptionally drawn followings, turned into a pivotal piece of powerhouse promoting. These powerhouses frequently have profound associations with their crowd and can apply a huge effect on their purchasing choices. This change in center towards miniature powerhouses was considered more credible and certified brand support, as it seemed like a suggestion from a companion as opposed to a big name underwriting.

The advancement of powerhouse showcasing likewise saw the ascent of specialty forces to be reckoned with. These are people who take care of profoundly unambiguous interests or networks, frequently with two or three thousand devotees. For brands, these powerhouses can be mother lodes, as they give admittance to an extremely designated and drawn in crowd.

As powerhouse advertising kept on developing, force to be reckoned with organizations and powerhouse commercial centers arose to smooth out the interaction. These stages associate brands with powerhouses, making it simpler to track down the ideal characters for explicit missions. This improvement professionalized the business, prompting better agreements, more clear assumptions, and more normalized remuneration.

One critical part of the development of force to be reckoned with advertising is the rising significance of legitimacy. Crowds have become savvier, and they can recognize a constrained or inauthentic brand underwriting far in advance. Subsequently, forces to be reckoned with and brands must be more straightforward and certified in their coordinated efforts to keep up with the trust of their supporters.

Notwithstanding validness, measurements and information investigation became essential to force to be reckoned with advertising. Brands could never again depend exclusively on the quantity of devotees a powerhouse had. All things being equal, they started to inspect commitment rates, transformation rates, and other execution measurements to decide the outcome of a mission. This information driven approach considered more proficient utilization of promoting financial plans and better return on initial capital investment.

The utilization of powerhouse promoting extended across ventures. It's not generally restricted to mold and magnificence brands. Powerhouses are currently unmistakable in businesses like travel, wellness, food, innovation, and even money.

The key is finding the right powerhouse for your specialty and crowd.

The new advancement of powerhouse advertising additionally integrates new stages and arrangements. TikTok, a short-video stage, has soar in ubiquity and has birthed another age of powerhouses.

Podcasting, as well, has set out open doors for powerhouses to interface with crowds in a more cozy, sound based setting.

In the realm of web based business, powerhouse promoting has flawlessly coordinated with the ascent of shoppable substance. Powerhouses can now tag and connect items straightforwardly in their posts, permitting devotees to make buys with a basic tap. This consistent shopping experience has made powerhouse advertising significantly more successful.

Guidelines and rules play likewise had an impact in forming the development of powerhouse showcasing. The Government Exchange Commission

(FTC) in the US and other administrative bodies overall have forced rules expecting powerhouses to reveal their associations and paid advancements. These guidelines plan to guarantee straightforwardness and safeguard purchasers from tricky publicizing rehearsals.

The advancement of powerhouse promoting isn't without challenges. Immersion in the market has prompted worries of genuineness, as some forces to be reckoned with resort to counterfeit supporters or commitment measurements.

Moreover, the expense of working with top-level powerhouses has soared, making it progressively challenging for more modest organizations to get to this advertising procedure.

In light of these difficulties, many brands have gone to nano-powerhouses - people with tiny yet exceptionally drew in followings. These powerhouses frequently charge lower expenses and can give a more grassroots, genuine association with nearby networks.

The future of force to be reckoned with promoting is probably going to be driven by additional mechanical advancements. Expanded reality (AR) and computer generated reality (VR) can possibly reshape the powerhouse scene by making vivid encounters for purchasers.

Computer based intelligence and AI devices will keep on refining the method involved with finding the ideal powerhouse for a mission.

The development of powerhouse showcasing is a demonstration of the unique idea of promoting business.

From the beginning of web gatherings to the ascent of nano-forces to be reckoned with and shoppable substance, this methodology has made considerable progress

Chapter 1
Identifying the Right Influencers

In the present advanced age, force to be reckoned with showcasing has turned into a basic piece of brand advancement and promoting procedures. Organizations are progressively going to powerhouses to associate with their interest group, assemble brand mindfulness, and drive deals. In any case, finding the right powerhouses for your image can be a complicated errand that requires a blend of workmanship and science. In this article, we'll investigate the critical elements to consider while distinguishing the right powerhouses for your showcasing efforts.

1. Characterize Your Objectives

Prior to plunging into the universe of force to be reckoned with, it's urgent to characterize your objectives plainly. What do you intend to accomplish with your powerhouse promoting effort? Might it be said that you are hoping to incrementally mark mindfulness, drive site traffic, support deals, or encourage commitment? Understanding your targets will assist you with recognizing powerhouses who line up with your objectives.

2. Know Your Interest group

Your interest group is at the center of powerhouse promoting. It's fundamental to have a profound comprehension of who your clients and they're keen on. This information will direct your choice of forces to be reckoned with who have a comparable crowd segment and interests. Search for powerhouses whose supporters match your ideal client profile.

3. Decide Your Specialty

Recognizing your specialty is vital in force to be reckoned with showcasing. You really want to pinpoint the particular business or classification in which your item or administration has a place. For instance, assuming you're in the wellness business, you ought to look for powerhouses who represent considerable authority in wellbeing and wellness. Niching down assists you with finding powerhouses who are specialists in your field and can associate with your interest group truly.

4. Think about Pertinence and Validness

Importance and genuineness are two of the most basic variables while picking forces to be reckoned with. A powerhouse who truly has faith in and utilizes your item or administration will seem to be more credible to their adherents. Realness is critical to building trust and validity. Guarantee that the powerhouses you select line up with your image's qualities and message.

5. Dissect Commitment Rates

It's not just about the quantity of adherents a powerhouse has; commitment rates matter as well. A powerhouse might have a tremendous following, however in the event that their crowd isn't effectively captivating with their substance, their effect on your showcasing effort might be restricted. See measurements like likes, remarks, and offers to check a powerhouse's degree of commitment with their crowd.

6. Check for Consistency

Consistency in happy quality and posting recurrence is one more fundamental perspective to consider. A powerhouse who routinely makes top notch content and keeps a steady posting plan is bound to keep their crowd locked in. Conflicting posting or a drop in satisfied quality could demonstrate an absence of responsibility, which could influence your mission's prosperity.

7. Survey Their Substance

Get some margin to survey a powerhouse's past satisfaction. Does their substance style and tone match your image's character and message? Search for any warnings, for example, questionable substance or a background marked by brand associations that might struggle with your qualities.

8. Survey Their Standing

Prior to joining forces with a powerhouse, research their web-based standing. Check for any regrettable press or contentions related to them. Powerhouses with a discolored standing can adversely influence your image's picture.

9. Investigate Their Joint efforts

Think about the powerhouses' past joint efforts. Have they worked with brands like yours? How effective were those missions? Understanding a powerhouse's history with different brands can give bits of knowledge into their capacity to successfully advance your items or administrations.

10. Arrange Terms and Pay

Whenever you've distinguished expected forces to be reckoned with, now is the ideal time to arrange the particulars of your organization. Examine remuneration, content creation, posting plan, and a particular necessities you have for the mission. A straightforward and commonly helpful understanding is urgent for a fruitful coordinated effort.

11. Screen and Measure Results

After your powerhouse advertising effort is in progress, be ready to screen and quantify the outcomes. Utilize key execution pointers (KPIs) pertinent to your objectives to evaluate the mission's prosperity. This could incorporate measurements like site traffic, deals, web-based entertainment development, and crowd commitment.

12. Fabricate Long haul Connections

Force to be reckoned with showcasing doesn't need to be a one-time commitment. Constructing long haul associations with the right powerhouses can be exceptionally useful. In the event that a powerhouse adjusts well to your image and conveys positive outcomes, consider broadening your coordinated effort past a solitary mission.

13. Adjust and Advance

The force to be reckoned with is ceaselessly developing. New stages, arising patterns, and changes in customer conduct can affect the viability of force to be reckoned with advertising. Keep awake to-date with these progressions and adjust your methodologies in like manner to stay pertinent and compelling.

Distinguishing the right powerhouses for your image is a blend of workmanship and science. It includes figuring out your objectives, interest group, and specialty, while additionally considering factors like significance, legitimacy, commitment rates, and a force to be reckoned with standing. By cautiously choosing powerhouses who line up with your image, you can make fruitful promoting efforts that resonate with your main interest group and drive genuine outcomes. Recall that powerhouse promotion is a unique field, and the capacity to adjust and develop your procedures is fundamental for long haul progress in this steadily changing computerized scene.

Defining Your Target Audience

The Way to Fruitful Correspondence

In the always developing scene of business and showcasing, one principal viewpoint stays consistent: the significance of understanding and characterizing your main interest group. Whether you're a growing business person or a deep rooted partnership, the outcome of your items or administrations relies on your capacity to recognize and interface with the right crowd. In this article, we will investigate the meaning of characterizing your ideal interest group and how to successfully go about it.

Why is Characterizing Your Interest group Urgent?

Accuracy in Correspondence: Knowing your interest group permits you to tailor your informing, content, and publicizing to their inclinations, needs, and interests. This accuracy in correspondence fundamentally improves the probability of catching their consideration and impacting them.

Asset Designation: Without a characterized crowd, you could squander significant assets on wide and incapable showcasing efforts. Characterizing your ideal interest group assists you with apportioning your spending plan and time all the more productively by zeroing in on individuals probably going to turn into your clients.

Building More grounded Connections: A profound comprehension of your interest group empowers you to fabricate more grounded, more private associations with them. At the point when clients feel like a brand comprehends and takes care of their particular requirements, they are bound to stay steadfast and advocate for your items or administrations.

Upper hand: In a serious commercial center, having the option to reach and associate with the right crowd gives you a critical benefit. It permits you to separate your image and contributions, separating you from the opposition.

Moves toward Characterize Your Ideal interest group:

Statistical surveying: Begin with intensive statistical surveying. Grasp the latest things in your industry, assemble information on shopper conduct, and recognize the socioeconomics and psychographics of possible clients. This underlying examination shapes the underpinning of your ideal interest group definition.

Demographics: Socioeconomics include essential attributes like age, orientation, area, training, and pay level. These subtleties assist you with making a fundamental profile of your optimal client.

Psychographics: Go past socioeconomics by digging into psychographics. This incorporates grasping the qualities, ways of life, interests, and yearnings of your crowd. Psychographics give bits of knowledge into why individuals settle on purchasing choices and what persuades them.

Social Variables: Examine the social elements of your crowd. This incorporates their buying propensities, brand devotion, and the issues or problem areas they're attempting to settle with your item or administration.

Segmentation: Whenever you have gathered this information, fragment your crowd into more modest, more reasonable gatherings. Each portion ought to have one of a kind qualities and inclinations that you can target independently.

Make Purchaser Personas: Foster point by point purchaser personas for each section. A purchaser persona is a semi-fictitious portrayal of your optimal client, including their name, age, work, family, side interests, and trouble spots. This makes it more straightforward to refine your crowd and make content that impacts them.

Serious Investigation: Figure out your rivals and their interest groups. This can assist you with recognizing holes on the lookout and regions where you can separate yourself.

Criticism and Overviews: Remember to assemble criticism straightforwardly from your current clients. Overviews, center gatherings, and online entertainment connections can give important experiences into their requirements and inclinations.

Test and Refine: Your main interest group definition isn't firmly established. As your business advances and the market changes, be ready to test and refine your crowd fragments. Ceaselessly reconsider your procedure to guarantee it stays powerful.

Pragmatic Models:

We should consider several functional guides to delineate the significance of characterizing your main interest group:

1. A Café

Assume you're the proprietor of a little café. Through statistical surveying, you find that your essential interest group is youthful experts aged 25-35 who work from a distance. They esteem a comfortable climate, great Wi-Fi, and excellent espresso. With this data, you can plan your shop, make a menu, and foster showcasing efforts that cater explicitly to this crowd. You could considerably offer devotion projects or limits during their pinnacle working hours to increment client maintenance.

2. A Product Organization

In the event that you run a product organization that works on efficient devices, you could observe that your essential crowd is little to medium-sized organizations hoping to smooth out their tasks. They esteem cost-productivity and convenience. By grasping these socioeconomics and psychographics, you can tweak your product highlights, estimating plans, and promoting materials to take care of this particular crowd's necessities and inclinations.

All in all, characterizing your ideal interest group isn't simply a showcasing exercise; it's an essential basis for any business. At the point when you have a reasonable comprehension of who your clients are, you can more readily adjust your items, administrations, and showcasing endeavors with their cravings and assumptions. This prompts expanded consumer loyalty, brand unwaveringly, and eventually, more prominent business achievement. In this way, carve out opportunities to characterize your ideal interest group, and watch your business flourish in the cutthroat market.

Micro-Influencers vs. Macro-Influencers

In the steadily developing scene of computerized showcasing, powerhouses have arisen as a strong power in advancing items, administrations, and thoughts. These powerhouses, with their significant internet based followings, can influence customer feelings and drive buying choices. Among powerhouses, two essential classifications have acquired noticeable quality: miniature forces to be reckoned with and large scale powerhouses. Every one of these classes enjoys its own one of a kind benefits and disadvantages, and picking between them is a pivotal choice for organizations trying to outfit the force of virtual entertainment.

Micro-Influencers: The Force of Validness

Miniature powerhouses, as the name proposes, are people with generally little yet exceptionally drew in virtual entertainment followings, regularly going from two or three thousand to a huge number of supporters. What separates miniature powerhouses is their capacity to interface with their crowd on an individual level, frequently described by trust, validity, and realness. These forces to be reckoned with commonly center around specialty regions, and their substance is in many cases revolved around their particular advantages or skill.

One of the essential benefits of working with miniature powerhouses is the realness they bring to their advancements. Their supporters view them as interesting people, not far off from big names, causing the underwriting of an item or administration to feel more real. This realness can prompt higher commitment rates, as supporters are bound to trust suggestions from miniature powerhouses.

Besides, miniature powerhouses are typically more savvy for organizations, as they frequently charge lower expenses for coordinated efforts contrasted with their full scale powerhouse partners. This moderateness is especially alluring to more modest organizations with restricted showcasing financial plans.

Miniature forces to be reckoned with can likewise convey a profoundly designated crowd. Since they frequently center around unambiguous specialties, organizations can work with miniature powerhouses whose devotees intently line up with their objective segment, guaranteeing that their message contacts the right crowd.

Macro-Influencers: The Compass and Star Power

Full scale forces to be reckoned with, then again, brag gigantic followings, frequently arriving at many thousands or even large numbers of supporters. These people have accomplished an elevated degree of notoriety and acknowledgment in the computerized world, and their substance can become a web sensation without sweat. Their allure lies in their wide reach and mass-market claim.

One of the vital advantages of working with full scale powerhouses is the sheer size of their crowd. Organizations can rapidly acquire openness to countless expected clients, which can be priceless for item dispatches or brand mindfulness crusades.

The immense reach of full scale powerhouses is particularly advantageous for enterprises where wide perceivability is fundamental.

Large scale powerhouses are likewise bound to have laid out associations with significant brands, which can lend credibility to organizations related to them. The star power and superstar status of large scale powerhouses can raise the apparent worth of an item or administration, making them especially alluring for top of the line or extravagance brands.

The Disadvantage of Each

Notwithstanding their benefits, both miniature powerhouses and large scale forces to be reckoned with have their drawbacks. For miniature powerhouses, the essential test is their restricted reach.

While their commitment rates might be high, their general crowd size is moderately little. This implies that organizations searching for mass openness may not find miniature powerhouses reasonable for their necessities.

Then again, full scale powerhouses, with their huge and various followings, may battle to keep up with the very level of vagueness and trust that miniature powerhouses have. Their supporters can once in a while seem to be more business and less private, which might prompt lower commitment and trust levels among their devotees.

Picking the Right Powerhouse for Your Business

The choice to work with miniature powerhouses or full scale forces to be reckoned with at last relies upon a business' particular objectives, interest group, and financial plan. Much of the time, a mix of both miniature and full scale forces to be reckoned with can be a powerful procedure.

For instance, a business could use the validity of miniature powerhouses for top to bottom item surveys and suggestions while involving large scale powerhouses for more extensive brand openness and high-influence crusades.

To settle on an educated decision, it's fundamental for organizations to direct careful exploration on likely powerhouses. This incorporates assessing their commitment rates, arrangement with brand values, and past joint efforts.

Furthermore, organizations ought to have a reasonable comprehension of their mission targets, whether it's driving deals, expanding brand mindfulness, or sending off another item.

All in all, the choice between miniature powerhouses and full scale forces to be reckoned with in the domain of computerized showcasing is a basic one. Every class has its novel assets and shortcomings, and the decision ought to be founded on the particular requirements and objectives of the business. No matter what the size of the powerhouse, the way into an effective force to be reckoned with promoting effort lies in the realness, importance, and reverberation between the force to be reckoned with, the brand, and the main interest group.

Tools and Strategies for Influencer Research

In the consistently developing scene of computerized promoting, powerhouse showcasing has arisen as a strong system to associate with interest groups. To outfit the maximum capacity of this methodology, it's vital to direct intensive powerhouse research. In this article, we'll dig into the devices and methodologies that can assist you with recognizing the right powerhouses for your image and missions.

Figuring out Powerhouse Exploration
Force to be reckoned with research is the essential move toward any powerhouse promoting effort. It includes the most common way of distinguishing, breaking down, and choosing powerhouses whose internet based presence lines up with your image's qualities and ideal interest group. This examination is fundamental to boost the effect of your advertising endeavors.

The Secrets to Success Online Entertainment Stages: The first and most essential device for powerhouse research is web-based entertainment stages themselves. By physically looking for important catchphrases, hashtags, or industry-related terms on stages like Instagram, YouTube, and Twitter, you can distinguish expected powerhouses.

Powerhouse Showcasing Stages: Different powerhouse advertising stages have arisen throughout the years to smooth out the examination interaction. Apparatuses like AspireIQ, Upfluence, and Traackr give admittance to broad force to be reckoned with data sets and high level pursuit channels to assist you with finding powerhouses in light of socio economics, interests, and commitment measurements.

Google Patterns: To distinguish moving subjects and possible powerhouses in a particular specialty, Google Patterns is an important device. It gives experiences into what individuals are looking for, assisting you with understanding which regions may be ready for powerhouse coordinated efforts.

BuzzSumo: This device permits you to find moving substances and persuasive people in a given field. It assists you with viewing as the most common substance connected with your industry, making it simpler to distinguish possible powerhouses.

Crowd Socioeconomics Apparatuses: Instruments like HypeAuditor and Social Edge can give important experiences into a force to be reckoned with. You can evaluate the validness of a powerhouse's following, view socioeconomics, and comprehend their commitment rates.

Force to be reckoned with Exploration Techniques Characterize Your Goals: Prior to leaving on powerhouse research, having clear goals for your campaign is indispensable. Characterize what you need to accomplish - whether it's image mindfulness, lead age, or deals - as this will direct your choice of forces to be reckoned with.

Distinguish Your Ideal interest group: Comprehend your main interest group's socioeconomics, interests, and ways of behaving. This will assist you with distinguishing powerhouses whose adherents line up with your expected clients.

Gather a Rundown of Likely Forces to be reckoned with: Utilize the devices referenced above to make a rundown of expected forces to be reckoned with. Think about both full scale powerhouses (those with an enormous following) and miniature powerhouses (who might have a more modest following yet more drawn in and specialty crowds).

Examine Content Quality: Take a gander at the substance a force to be reckoned with produces. Is it lined up with your image's qualities and style? Does it reverberate with your ideal interest group? Top notch content is essential for a fruitful powerhouse organization.

Really take a look at Commitment Measurements: Commitment rates are much of the time more significant than devotee count. Examine a powerhouse's preferences, remarks, and offers to measure how well they interface with their crowd. Higher commitment demonstrates a more devoted and involved fan base.

Survey Realness: Use instruments like HypeAuditor to guarantee the legitimacy of a powerhouse's following. Counterfeit adherents can expand a powerhouse's numbers yet will not offer genuine benefit to your mission.

Assess Powerhouse Notoriety: Research a powerhouse's standing. Are there any contentions or negative affiliations that could inadequately ponder your image assuming you team up with them?

Connect and Construct Connections: In the wake of distinguishing likely forces to be reckoned with, now is the ideal time to connect. It is fundamental to Lay out a relationship. This should be possible through customized messages, email effort, or utilizing powerhouse promoting stages for presentations.

Arrange Terms and Arrangements: Whenever you've distinguished the right forces to be reckoned with and have laid out an association, arrange the conditions of the organization. Obviously characterize assumptions, expectations, pay, and any selectiveness conditions.

Track and Examine Results: After the force to be reckoned with showcasing effort is live, consistently screen and track the outcomes. Use devices like Google Examination, virtual entertainment bits of knowledge, and following connections to evaluate the effect of the cooperation on your image's objectives.

All in all, powerhouse research is a principal part of force to be reckoned with showcasing. The instruments and techniques referenced here engage advertisers to find the right powerhouses, they are compelling and effective to guarantee their missions. By characterizing targets, utilizing fitting instruments, and building associations with powerhouses, brands can take

advantage of the force of this dynamic
and compelling type of promoting

Chapter 2 Developing an Influencer Marketing Strategy

In the realm of advanced advertising,
scarcely any procedures have acquired
as much noticeable quality and
accomplishment as powerhouse
promoting. This approach uses the force
of people who have developed a
committed following via web-based
entertainment stages to advance items,
administrations, or brands. To make a
successful powerhouse showcasing
system, one should think about different
perspectives, from recognizing the right
powerhouses to creating a convincing
effort that lines up with your image's
goal. We will dive into the critical stages
in fostering an effective powerhouse
showcasing technique.

Characterize Your Targets
Prior to jumping into the universe of
powerhouse advertising, characterizing
your objectives is fundamental. What
are you planning to accomplish through
this technique? Shared objectives
incorporate expanding brand

mindfulness, driving site traffic, supporting deals, or creating client produced content. Realizing your targets will direct your powerhouse determination and mission approach.

Recognize Your Interest group

Understanding your main interest group is basic in powerhouse advertising. You should adjust the force to be reckoned with crowd to your image's optimal clients. Examine socio economics, interests, and online ways of behaving to find powerhouses who can reach and draw in your ideal buyer base really.

Research and Recognize Forces to be reckoned with: When you know your goals and interest group, now is the right time to recognize likely forces to be reckoned with. There are different apparatuses and stages accessible to aid this interaction. Search for powerhouses who are pertinent to your industry as well as have a certifiable association with their devotees. Miniature powerhouses, those with more modest but exceptionally drawn in followings, can frequently yield noteworthy outcomes.

Assess Powerhouse Genuineness

In the period of force to be reckoned with promoting, realness is vital. Guarantee the forces to be reckoned with are really intrigued by your item or administration and can give legitimate, unprejudiced audits. Crowds can recognize inauthentic supports far in advance, which can harm your image's standing.

Lay out Your Spending plan

Force to be reckoned with advertising can shift fundamentally in cost. Big name powerhouses order high expenses, while miniature forces to be reckoned with are more financial plan agreeable. Decide your financial plan in view of your targets, and be ready to designate assets for powerhouse pay as well as for content creation, following, and examination.

Make a Far reaching Understanding

Whenever you've picked your powerhouses, drafting an unmistakable and thorough agreement is significant. This arrangement ought to frame the extent of work, expectations, installment terms, and any lawful necessities or exposure guidelines. A straightforward organization is vital to a fruitful powerhouse showcasing effort.

Foster Connecting with Content

Content is at the core of force to be reckoned with advertising. Team up with powerhouses to make content that reverberates with their crowd while advancing your image. Content can take many structures, from supported presents on Instagram on YouTube item audits, blog entries, or even live-streamed occasions. The substance ought to line up with your image's information and be introduced in a drawing in a valid way.

Execute a Global positioning framework

To quantify the outcome of your force to be reckoned with showcasing effort, carry out a global positioning framework that screens key execution pointers (KPIs). These may incorporate measurements like commitment rates, navigate rates, transformation rates, and the general effect on your image's targets. Different examination apparatuses are accessible to help you track and assess the presentation of your mission.

Screen and Change

Force to be reckoned with promoting is definitely not a limited time offer technique. Ceaselessly screen your mission's exhibition and be ready to make changes on a case by case basis. This could incorporate changing the substance approach, focusing on various forces to be reckoned with, or in any event, turning your mission goals in view of constant information.

Construct Long haul Connections

While powerhouse showcasing can be an oddball joint effort, it frequently pays to construct long haul associations with forces to be reckoned with who really resonate with your image. Long haul associations can prompt expanded trust and validity with the powerhouse's crowd and can give reliable openness to your items or administrations.

Guarantee Revelation and Consistency

Powerhouse promoting is dependent upon guidelines and rules that require divulgence of paid associations or supported content. Ensure your powerhouses know about these guidelines and comply with them. Rebelliousness can prompt legitimate issues and harm your image's standing.

Influence Client Created Content

Notwithstanding force to be reckoned with produced content, energize client created content (UGC). At the point when clients share their positive encounters with your item or administration via virtual entertainment, this can be a strong support. Repost UGC on your image's social channels to make a feeling of the local area and trust.

Investigate and Learn

After the mission is finished, investigate the information and results completely. What worked? What didn't really? Utilize the experiences acquired from the mission to illuminate your future powerhouse promoting endeavors. Ceaseless improvement is fundamental in the quickly developing scene of computerized promoting.

All in all, powerhouse promoting is a dynamic and compelling system when executed mindfully. By characterizing clear targets, recognizing the right forces to be reckoned with, making convincing substance, and constantly breaking down and changing your methodology, you can bridle the force of powerhouse advertising to successfully advance your image. With the right powerhouses and a very much created system, you can interface with your ideal interest group truly and accomplish your showcasing objectives.

Setting Clear Goals and Objective

The Diagram for Progress

Defining clear objectives and goals is the foundation of making progress, whether in private or expert undertakings. These objectives act as a guide that guides us, giving guidance and motivation to our activities. In this 700-word investigation, we will dig into the significance of putting forth clear objectives and goals, the advantages they bring, and how to actually make and oversee them.

Why Define Clear Objectives and Targets?

Clearness and Concentration: Laying out clear objectives and goals assists people and associations with acquiring lucidity about what they need to accomplish. It gives a laser-sharp spotlight on what should be finished and where to contribute time and assets. Without this lucidity, endeavors can become dispersed and wasteful.

Inspiration and Motivation: Having distinct objectives can be a strong wellspring of inspiration. At the point when we have an unmistakable image of what we're pursuing, it can motivate us to beat difficulties and continue onward, even despite mishaps.

Estimating Progress: Objectives go about as achievements, empowering us to quantify our advancement. They permit us to follow our presentation and decide if we're moving in the correct bearing. This estimation helps in making vital acclimations to remain on track.

Accountability: Clear objectives give a premise to responsibility. At the point when goals are set, it's more straightforward to relegate liabilities and figure out who is answerable for what. This upgrades responsibility and guarantees that everybody knows their job.

Prioritization: Objectives help in focusing on undertakings and tasks. At the point when we set goals, we can separate between what's generally significant and what's less basic. This guides in apportioning assets successfully and zeroing in on high-influence exercises.

Upgraded Direction: Laying out clear objectives settles on choice making more direct. At the point when we understand what we're attempting to accomplish, we can assess choices in view of how well they line up with our targets, pursuing it simpler to settle on choices that help our objectives.

The Advantages of Defining Clear Objectives and Goals

Further developed Execution: One of the main benefits of clear objectives is further developed execution. At the point when people and groups understand what they are really going after, they will quite often perform better as they are spurred to accomplish their goals.

Efficiency: Objectives and goals smooth out the work process. By recognizing what should be achieved, assignments and exercises become more coordinated and effective. This can save time and assets.

Better Correspondence: Clear objectives encourage better correspondence inside groups and associations. At the point when everybody is in total agreement about the thing they are attempting to accomplish, it prompts more powerful joint effort.

Self-improvement: Defining individual objectives can prompt self-improvement and advancement. Whether it's mastering another expertise or taking on a better way of life, setting clear goals can be an incredible asset for personal growth.

Advancement and Imagination: Objectives can likewise rouse advancement and innovativeness. At the point when individuals are tested to accomplish something explicit, they frequently concoct effective fixes and thoughts to arrive at those objectives.

Instructions to Lay out Clear Objectives and Targets

Be Explicit: Objectives ought to be explicit and distinct. Rather than saying, "I need to find success," say, "I need to expand my deals by 20% in the following quarter." Explicit objectives are simpler to pursue.

Measurable: Objectives ought to be quantifiable. This implies you ought to have the option to evaluate your advancement. For instance, assuming you want to get more fit, indicate the number of pounds you expect to lose.

Achievable: Guarantee that your objectives are feasible. They ought to be sensible and reachable. Defining unreachable objectives can prompt disappointment and demotivation.

Relevant: Objectives ought to be pertinent to your general goals. Assuming you're laying out vocation objectives, they ought to line up with your drawn out profession plans.

Time-Bound: Each objective ought to have a cutoff time. This adds a need to get moving and assists you with keeping focused. Without a time period, there's a gamble of dawdling.

Get Them On paper: Explicitly stating your objectives makes them more unmistakable. It's a guarantee to yourself or your association. Keep your composed objectives where you can consistently audit them.

Overseeing Clear Objectives and Goals

Defining clear objectives is only the initial step. It is similarly essential to Oversee them.

Ordinary Survey: Ceaselessly audit your objectives. Survey your headway and make fundamental changes. Could it be said that you are on target? Do you have to change your methodology?

Separate into Errands: Objectives can frequently be separated into more modest errands or achievements. This makes the way to accomplishing the objective not so much overpowering but rather more sensible.

Observe Accomplishments: At the point when you arrive at an objective, regardless of how little, praise your accomplishment. Recognizing your victories can lift inspiration and a feeling of confidence.

Gain from Misfortunes: Not all objectives will be accomplished without misfortunes. At the point when you experience impediments, make a move to learn and adjust your system.

All in all, putting forth clear objectives and goals is definitely not a simple convention, however a crucial part of outcome in any part of life. Whether you are chasing after a vocation, working on your own life, or dealing with an association, having obvious objectives gives a guide to direct your endeavors. Objectives offer lucidity, inspiration, and a way to quantify progress. By sticking to the standards of putting forth and overseeing clear objectives, people and associations can accomplish their yearnings and dreams.

Crafting a Compelling Brand Message

In a world soaked with commercials and data, making a convincing brand message has turned into a central test for organizations. Your image message is the quintessence of your organization's personality and the foundation of your advertising system. A strong brand message can slice through the commotion, catch the consideration of your main interest group, and have an enduring impression. In this article, we will investigate the specialty of making a convincing brand message that resounds with your crowd and drives your business forward.

Grasping Your Image

Before you can create a convincing brand message, you really want to have a profound comprehension of your image's character. This goes past your items or administrations. Your image includes your organization's qualities, mission, and culture. Ask yourself, "What does our image depend on? What are our center standards and convictions? What separates us from the opposition?"A persuasive message is supported by an understandable perception of the personality of your picture.

Recognize the potential perspectives of your listeners.

Your image message ought to be intended to reverberate with your interest group. To do this, you should understand who your listeners' perspective is, what they are worth, and what challenges they face. Statistical surveying is significant in such a manner. Make itemized client personas and distinguish their problem areas. What keeps them up around evening time? What arrangements would they say they are searching for? Your image message ought to talk straightforwardly to these requirements.

Effortlessness and Lucidity

The best brand messages are basic and clear. Your crowd ought to grasp your message initially. Consider Nike's notorious slogan, "Take care of business." This compact assertion embodies the brand's ethos of strengthening and activity. Keep away from language and complex language. All things being equal, center around clear, important expressions that embody your image's embodiment.

Separation

Your image message ought to convey what makes your organization extraordinary. What separates you from the opposition? Whether it's a one of a kind item including outstanding client support, or a surprising history, your image message ought to feature what pursues you the better decision. For instance, Apple's message has for quite some time been focused on development and configuration, separating them in the tech business.

Feeling and Narrating

Convincing brand messages summon feelings. Individuals don't recollect raw numbers, yet they really do recall how a brand caused them to feel. Narrating is an incredible asset for accomplishing this. Share tales that reflect the goals and values of your brand. Airbnb's "Have a place Anyplace" crusade, for example, recounts accounts of individuals discovering a feeling of having a place in new spots, making a profound association with the brand.

Consistency Across Channels

Your image message ought to be predictable across all channels and touchpoints. Whether it's your site, web-based entertainment, print materials, or client communications, the message ought to stay uniform. This consistency supports your image's character and assembles entrust with your crowd. Irregularities can befuddle and distance possible clients.

Realness

The present purchasers are profoundly sensitive to validness. They can recognize a deceitful brand message well in advance. Your message ought to line up with your activities and values as an organization. Genuineness constructs trust and long haul devotion. Patagonia, for instance, is eminent for its bona fide obligation to ecological maintainability, which is profoundly implanted in their image message and practices.

Adaptability

While consistency is fundamental, your image message ought to likewise be sufficiently adaptable to adjust to evolving conditions. Your business might develop, and the market can move. Your message ought to have the option to turn when essential without losing its center personality. For example, during the Coronavirus pandemic, many organizations changed their image messages to reflect compassion and backing for clients, showing their versatility.

Visual and Verbal Marking

Your image message ought to be built up by your visual and verbal marking. This incorporates your logo, variety plan, typography, and voice. These components ought to line up with your image message, making a firm and critical brand insight. Consider Coca-Cola's unmistakable red and white logo, which supplements its message of satisfaction and reward.

Criticism and Testing

Making a convincing brand message is a continuous interaction. It's vital for accumulate criticism and lead testing to guarantee your message is reverberating with your crowd. Use reviews, center gatherings, and information investigation to gauge the viability of your message and make essential changes.

Instances of Convincing Brand Messages

A few brands have excelled at creating convincing brand messages:
Apple: " Think Unique" - This message addresses development and singularity.
Coca-Cola: " Open Joy" - It associates the brand with positive feelings.
Dove: " Genuine Magnificence" - Pigeon's message centers around advancing fearlessness and realness.
Google: " Try not to Be Malevolent" (previously) - This message underlined corporate morals and making the best decision.
All in all, making a convincing brand message is a fragile yet fundamental

errand for any business. It's about what you offer as well as about how you cause your clients to feel and the qualities you maintain. A convincing brand message is the extension that interfaces your image with your crowd, making an enduring and significant relationship. It ought to be basic, credible, and genuinely thunderous, while likewise separating your image from the opposition. Recollect that your image message isn't static - it ought to develop and adjust as your business and the market change.

Choosing the Right Social Media Platforms

In the computerized age, online entertainment has turned into a vital piece of our lives. Whether you're a singular hoping to remain associated with loved ones or a business intending to extend its span, online entertainment stages offer a variety of chances. In any case, with so many stages accessible, it tends to be trying to conclude which ones are ideal for your particular objectives. In this period of data over-burden, picking the right web-based entertainment stages is pivotal for successful correspondence and showcasing.

The most vital phase in settling on the best decision is to characterize your targets. Is it true or not that you are hoping to advance your business, construct an individual brand, or basically keep in contact with friends and family? Realizing your objectives will direct you in choosing the suitable stages. Here, we'll investigate different elements to consider while picking the right virtual entertainment stages.

Interest group:

Understanding your main interest group is fundamental. Different online entertainment stages draw in unmistakable socioeconomics. For instance, in the event that you're focusing on a more youthful crowd, stages like TikTok and Snapchat may be more reasonable. Interestingly, Facebook will in general allure for a more seasoned segment. Consider who you need to reach, and afterward pick stages that line up with that crowd.

Content Sort:

The kind of happiness you plan to make assumes an essential part in stage determination. In the event that you intend to share long-structured articles or recordings, stages like YouTube or Medium may be great. For short, captivating substance, stages like Instagram and Twitter are seriously fitting. Your substance methodology ought to line up with the stage's assets.

Industry and Specialty:

Think about your industry and specialty. Certain enterprises might have explicit stages where they flourish. For example, LinkedIn is an essential decision for experts and B2B organizations, while design and way of life organizations frequently flourish with Instagram. Research where your rivals and friends are dynamic to acquire bits of knowledge into the best stages for your industry.

Time and Assets:

Overseeing web-based entertainment records can time-consume. Every stage requires predictable commitment to keep up with significance. Be reasonable about the time and assets you can devote to virtual entertainment. It's smarter to succeed on two or three stages than to extend yourself excessively far across many.

Stage Highlights:

Various stages offer extraordinary elements and apparatuses. For instance, Instagram underscores visual substance and stories, while LinkedIn is intended for proficient systems administration and sharing industry-related articles. Get to know these elements and pick stages that line up with your substance and correspondence style.

Brand Persona:

Your image's character and values ought to line up with the stage's way of life. On the off chance that you're a fun loving and imaginative brand, TikTok might be a solid match. For a more serious and proficient picture, LinkedIn or Twitter may be better. Consistency in brand persona across stages is fundamental for a solid web-based presence.

Examination and Information:

Admittance to examination and information is vital for estimating the progress of your web-based entertainment endeavors. A few stages offer hearty experiences and revealing instruments, while others have restricted choices. Assuming following execution is really important, pick stages that give the information you really want to examine your methodology.

Competition:
Dissect your opposition's web-based entertainment presence. Recognize which stages they use and survey their methodologies. This can give significant bits of knowledge into where your interest group is dynamic and the way in which you can separate your methodology.

Patterns and Calculation Changes:
Remain informed about the steadily developing scene of virtual entertainment. Stages as often as possible update their calculations and present new elements. Stay aware of these progressions and change your technique in a manner to stay applicable and boost commitment.

Test and Adjust:
Picking the right web-based entertainment stages is certainly not a one-time choice. It's a continuous interaction. Be available to test various stages and systems. Break down the outcomes and adjust your methodology in light of what turns out best for your objectives.

All in all, choosing the right web-based entertainment stages is an essential choice that requires conscious thought. Your decision ought to be directed by your goals, interest group, content sort, industry, assets, stage highlights, brand persona, information access, rivalry, and versatility to evolving patterns. By pursuing informed choices, you can actually bridle the force of web-based entertainment to associate with your crowd and accomplish your objectives. Keep in mind, there's actually no need to focus on being all over the place, however being where it makes the biggest difference.

Chapter 3 Collaboration and Partnerships

In the present interconnected and quickly developing world, cooperation and associations have become fundamental procedures for outcome in different areas, from business and training to medical services and global strategy. The familiar saying, "Two heads are superior to one," turns out as expected as associations and people perceive the force of cooperating to accomplish shared objectives. In this 800-word investigation, we will dig into the meaning of coordinated effort and associations, the various structures they can take, and their effect on development, critical thinking, and generally progress.

The Force of Cooperation

Cooperation is the most common way of cooperating with people or gatherings to accomplish a common objective. It has been at the core of human advancement for a really long time. Whether it's researchers working together on weighty examination, performers making amicable songs, or organizations fashioning key partnerships, cooperation is an essential driver of development and development.

One of the vital benefits of coordinated effort is the variety of viewpoints it brings. At the point when individuals from various foundations, disciplines, or abilities meet up, they offer remarkable bits of knowledge and abilities that would be useful. This variety sparkles imagination and development, cultivating novel thoughts and arrangements that probably won't have arisen in a siloed climate.

Coordinated effort is additionally fundamental in tending to complex difficulties. Whether it's handling worldwide issues like environmental change, destitution, or pandemics, or taking care of issues inside an association, the pooling of assets and information is in many cases the best method for tracking down arrangements. It advances aggregate critical thinking, drawing on the qualities and mastery of every giver.

Types of Cooperation

Cooperation can take different structures, each custom-made to the particular requirements and targets of the gatherings in question. Here are a few normal kinds of coordinated effort:

Vital Organizations: In the business world, organizations frequently structure vital associations to accomplish common advantages. These associations can incorporate joint endeavors, co-advertising arrangements, or long haul joint efforts pointed toward growing business sector reach, sharing assets, or driving development.

Cross-Disciplinary Joint effort: In the areas of science, innovation, and the scholarly community, cross-disciplinary cooperation is predominant. Scientists from various foundations meet up to resolve complex issues that require a mix of skills. For instance, clinical analysts team up with specialists to foster high level medical care arrangements.

Worldwide Participation: On the worldwide stage, nations coordinate on different issues, like economic accords, security partnerships, and ecological arrangements. Global associations like the Unified Countries give a stage to conciliatory coordinated effort to address overall difficulties.

Local area Joint effort: At the nearby level, local area associations and people team up to work on their areas, schools, or public administrations. These endeavors can include humanitarian effort, raising support, or backing.

The Job of Innovation

In the computerized age, innovation has changed the manner in which we work together. Specialized devices, for example, video conferencing, informing applications, and task board programming, have made it simpler for people and associations to interface and work together, paying little mind to geological distance.

The Coronavirus pandemic sped up the reception of far off cooperation, compelling numerous to adjust to virtual workplaces. While this change had its difficulties, it likewise featured the versatility and flexibility of people and associations. Distant coordinated effort supported business tasks as well as opened up new open doors for worldwide ability procurement and cooperation.

Besides, the ascent of open-source programming and information sharing stages has democratized joint effort. Networks of engineers, researchers, and aficionados overall team up on open-source projects, adding to developments that are available to all. This open methodology has prompted the advancement of innovations like Linux, Wikipedia, and innumerable others.

Difficulties of Coordinated effort

While coordinated effort offers various advantages, it isn't without its difficulties. Powerful joint effort requires clear correspondence, trust, and a common vision. Misconceptions or clashes can emerge when these components are inadequate. Moreover, overseeing assorted groups with various societies, time regions, and working styles can be intricate.

One more test in cooperation is the best potential for one party to overwhelm or take advantage of the relationship. In associations between associations or nations, power irregular characteristics can prompt inconsistent advantages. Straightforwardness and decency are significant to guarantee that all gatherings included benefit impartially from the joint effort.

Influence on Development

Coordinated effort and organizations are impetuses for advancement. At the point when various personalities meet up, they bring new viewpoints, thoughts, and abilities to the table. This cross-fertilization of information frequently prompts noteworthy advancements that can possibly change ventures and work on individuals' lives.

Development isn't restricted to the innovation area. It stretches out to fields like medical care, where coordinated efforts between drug organizations, research establishments, and medical care suppliers lead to the advancement of new medications, therapies, and clinical innovations. It additionally applies to the inventive expressions, where coordinated efforts between performers, craftsmen, and authors produce magnum opuses that resound with crowds around the world.

Cooperation and associations are something beyond popular expressions; they are the foundations of outcome in our interconnected world. Whether you are a business chief, a specialist, a local area coordinator, or a representative, perceiving the force of cooperation can open new doors and arrangements. Through a variety of thought, shared goals, and the utilization of innovation, joint effort impels advancement and critical thinking higher than ever. Embracing cooperation, while exploring its difficulties, is fundamental for people and associations the same as we keep on handling the mind boggling issues within recent memory and prepare for a more promising time to come.

Building Relationships with Influencers

In the always developing scene of advertising and brand advancement, building associations with powerhouses has turned into an important procedure. Powerhouse promoting uses the scope and validity of people who have amassed significant followings via web-based entertainment or other advanced stages. These powerhouses employ the ability to influence the suppositions and choices of their devotees, making them a strong power in the realm of showcasing. To tackle this potential, brands should have serious areas of strength for fashion true associations with powerhouses. In this article, we will investigate the significance of powerhouse connections and proposition common sense experiences into how to assemble and keep up with them.

The Ascent of Force to be reckoned with Showcasing

The ascent of force to be reckoned with showcasing can be credited to the changing idea of shopper conduct and the advanced age. Customers today are more suspicious of conventional promoting techniques and look for realness in the brands they draw in with. Powerhouses, with their own accounts and certifiable proposals, are viewed as reliable wellsprings of data.

Powerhouse advertising includes different structures, from superstar supporters to miniature forces to be reckoned with who have more modest yet exceptionally drew in crowds. The ongoing idea among these methodologies is the special interaction that powerhouses have with their adherents. This association makes force to be reckoned with advertising so successful.

Why Building Connections Matters

Building associations with powerhouses is fundamental in light of multiple factors. Most importantly, it guarantees legitimacy in the powerhouse's support. A certifiable connection between a brand and a force to be reckoned with brings about additional reasonable and convincing substance. At the point when powerhouses really trust in an item or administration, their supports are more genuine, which reverberates with their crowd.

Furthermore, solid associations with powerhouses can prompt long haul organizations. As opposed to one-off advancements, brands can team up with powerhouses on a continuous premise. This not just saves time and assets on tracking down new powerhouses for each mission yet additionally considers more inside and out, real narrating about the brand.

Moves toward Fabricate Associations with Powerhouses

Exploration and Choice: The most important phase in building associations with powerhouses is to find the perfect people who line up with your image's qualities and interest group. Search for powerhouses whose substance and individual brand reverberate with your item or administration.

Engagement: Draw in with the powerhouse's substance by loving, remarking, and sharing. Show real interest in their work. This step lays out an association and makes you noticeable to the powerhouse.

Outreach: Contact powerhouses with a customized message. Keep away from conventional, layout driven messages. All things being equal, express your deference for their work and your advantage in a likely joint effort.

Offer Worth: While moving toward forces to be reckoned with, offering some incentive is critical. Offer an unmistakable recommendation that frames how the coordinated effort will help the two players. Whether it's through financial pay, free items, or openness, make it a mutually beneficial arrangement.

Fabricate Trust: Building trust is fundamental in powerhouse connections. Be straightforward about your image's targets and assumptions. It's additionally critical to permit powerhouses artistic liberty, as their genuineness draws in their crowd.

Open Correspondence: Keep up with open lines of correspondence with powerhouses all through the organization. Ordinary registrations, input, and updates are fundamental. This guarantees that the two players are adjusted and happy with the coordinated effort.

Show Appreciation: Show appreciation for the powerhouse's work and the effect they have on your image. Perceive their endeavors through authentic appreciation and, when proper, little tokens of appreciation.

Long haul Responsibility: Building associations with powerhouses is definitely not a one-time try. Consider laying out long haul organizations where the two players become together. This approach encourages further associations and trust over the long haul.

Challenges in Building Force to be reckoned with Connections

Building associations with powerhouses isn't without its difficulties. It demands investment, exertion, and an eagerness to adjust. A few normal difficulties include:

Saturation: The powerhouse showcasing scene has become soaked, making it more testing to stick out and shape significant associations with powerhouses.

Authenticity: Keeping up with legitimacy in powerhouse associations can be troublesome, particularly on the off chance that powerhouses work together with various brands at the same time.

Evolving Calculations: Online entertainment stages every now and again change their calculations, affecting the compass and commitment of powerhouse content. Brands and forces to be reckoned with should adjust to these changes.

Lawful and Moral Contemplations: Guaranteeing that powerhouse organizations conform to lawful and moral guidelines, like divulgence of paid advancements, is fundamental.

Building associations with powerhouses is a central system for brands in the present computerized promoting scene. These connections, when sustained genuinely, can prompt more compelling showcasing efforts, expanded brand trust, and long haul associations. By leading intensive exploration, offering esteem, and keeping up with open correspondence, brands can use the force of powerhouse promoting to reach and resonate with their main interest groups. Be that as it may, it's pivotal to recognize the difficulties and stay versatile as the powerhouse promoting scene keeps on advancing.

Negotiating Terms and Compensation

Arranging the terms and remuneration of a proposition for employment is an essential move toward the business cycle. It's the place where a likely representative and boss get together to decide the states of their expert relationship. This discussion can altogether affect your profession, work fulfillment, and monetary prosperity. In this article, we will investigate the critical parts of arranging terms and pay, offering experiences and tips to assist you with exploring this significant cycle successfully.

1. Know Your Value

Prior to going into discussions, it's fundamental to comprehend your own worth in the gig market. Research what experts in comparable jobs, ventures, and areas are procuring. Various web-based assets and compensation studies can give you a sensible reach for your situation. Moreover, consider your experience, abilities, and capabilities.

This information will act as the establishment for your discussion system.

2. Focus on Remuneration Components

Remuneration isn't restricted to only the base compensation. There are different components to consider, including rewards, investment opportunities, benefits, and different advantages. Contemplate what means quite a bit to you and your monetary security. On the off chance that you have specific monetary objectives, for example, putting something aside for a home or taking care of educational loans, you might need to focus on a higher base compensation. Then again, on the off chance that you esteem balance between fun and serious activities, you could focus on extra get-away days or remote work choices.

3. Think about the Entire Bundle

The exchange cycle isn't just about what you procure yet what you keep. Focus on the expense suggestions and different allowances that will influence your salary. It's essential to think about long haul benefits, for example, retirement plans, medical services, and vocation improvement potential open doors. A task with a somewhat lower compensation yet brilliant advantages may be more important over the long haul.

4. Timing Is Vital

Arranging remuneration isn't exclusively about the second you get a proposition for employment. It tends to be a progression of discussions all through the recruiting system. First, center around laying out your fit for the job and the organization. When the business has communicated areas of strength for you, you can move into conversations about pay. Try not to race into this stage. Allow the business to take the principal action, if conceivable.

5. Be Proficient and Deferential

At the point when it comes time to arrange, impressive skill is significant. Move toward the discussion with deference and a helpful demeanor. You and your potential manager ought to consider the discussion to be a common work to arrive at an understanding that fulfills the two players. Try not to set expectations and ultimatums, as this can harm the relationship before it even starts.

6. Practice Compelling Correspondence

Solid relational abilities are central during exchange. Obviously express your assumptions and thinking for the terms you propose. Undivided attention is similarly significant; focus on the business' interests and be prepared to address them. Keep in mind, it's about what you say as well as how you say it. Being understandable, sure, and political can assist you with presenting major areas of strength for your ideal terms.

7. Be Adaptable

Exchange frequently includes split the difference. While it's fundamental for know your value and promoter for your requirements, being available to flexibility is similarly significant. Think about the business' imperatives and the general advantages of the gig.

Once in a while, an organization will most likely be unable to meet your underlying compensation demand, however they could offer other significant advantages, for example, extra took care of or expert improvement of valuable open doors.

8. Know When to Leave

At times, regardless of your earnest attempts, you may not arrive at an arrangement that lines up with your necessities and values. It's significant to perceive when now is the right time to leave.

In the event that a potential business is reluctant to offer sensible remuneration or is unyielding in talks, it very well may be an indication of future troubles. Keep in mind, the exchange cycle isn't only for the business' advantage, yet additionally for you to guarantee that you're entering a fair and satisfying work relationship.

9. Record Everything

All through the discussion interaction, track all correspondence. This incorporates messages, notes from discussions, and any settled upon terms. Having a put down account can assist with keeping away from errors and guarantee that the two players satisfy their responsibilities.

10. Look for Proficient Counsel

In the event that you're dubious about the exchange cycle, it tends to be useful to talk with a profession guide or a lawyer to spend significant time in work regulation. They can give master direction and assist you with exploring complex dealings.

All in all, arranging terms and remuneration is a significant stage in getting some work that lines up with your profession objectives and monetary requirements. A cycle requests planning, compelling correspondence, and a readiness to be adaptable while keeping up with your self-esteem.

By moving toward exchanges expertly and consciously, you can build your possibilities of getting a pay bundle that fulfills both you and your likely boss. Keep in mind, it's not just about the compensation; about making a commonly valuable work relationship upholds your professional development and generally prosperity.

Legal and Ethical Considerations

In the present quickly developing world, lawful and moral contemplations assume a significant part in shaping our social orders, organizations, and individual lives. Understanding the complexities of these contemplations isn't just important for consistency yet additionally for encouraging a fair and dependable society. This exposition dives into the key lawful and moral contemplations that have become progressively conspicuous in contemporary society.

One of the premier legitimate contemplations in the advanced age is information security. With the multiplication of computerized advances and the web, individual data is more open and defenseless than any time in recent memory. Legislatures overall have perceived the significance of information security and ordered regulations like the European Association's Overall Information Assurance Guideline (GDPR) and the

California Customer Protection Act (CCPA) in the US to defend people's very own information. These guidelines safeguard the security of people as well as consider organizations responsible for information breaks and abuse.

Moral contemplations with regards to information protection are similarly critical. Organizations gathering and taking care of individual information ought to embrace moral practices by acquiring informed assent, guaranteeing information security, and being straightforward about how the information will be utilized. Moral information dealing with standards additionally incorporates not oppressing people in light of their information, which can prompt unreasonable results, for example, one-sided calculations in employing or loaning processes.

Another key lawful and moral thought spins around ecological maintainability. Even with environmental change and natural debasement, regulations and moral rules have arisen to battle these difficulties. States overall are carrying out natural guidelines, for example, fossil fuel byproduct cutoff points and waste administration strategies. These regulations mean to decrease the adverse consequence of human exercises on the climate and safeguard regular assets for people in the future.

The moral component of ecological maintainability goes past simple consistency with regulations. It involves an ethical obligation to safeguard the planet and its biological systems. Moral contemplations include organizations embracing reasonable works on, monitoring assets, and limiting their carbon impression. Also, people are urged to diminish, reuse, and reuse to limit their biological effect.

A basic legitimate and moral worry that has acquired conspicuousness in contemporary society is civil rights. Issues connected with racial, orientation, and monetary disparity have provoked developments and conversations on equity and equity. Regulations have been instituted to address separation and advance value, like the enemy of segregation regulations, governmental policy regarding minorities in society approaches, and equivalent compensation guidelines.

Moral contemplations in the domain of civil rights stretch out to perceiving the intrinsic poise and worth, everything being equal, regardless of their experience or personality. This incorporates advancing variety and consideration, testing generalizations, and supporting fair treatment in all circles of life. Additionally, moral standards require recognizing authentic shameful acts and making progress toward compromise and restitutions now and again.

The approach of innovation and the advanced age has brought about new legitimate and moral difficulties connected with man-made reasoning (computer based intelligence) and mechanization. The utilization of simulated intelligence in dynamic cycles, such as employing or loaning, raises worries about predisposition and decency. Lawful structures are arising to resolve these issues, for example, the Fair Credit Announcing Act in the US.

Moral contemplations in man-made intelligence envelop guaranteeing straightforwardness in calculations, tending to predisposition in information and dynamic cycles, and creating components for responsibility when simulated intelligence frameworks make blunders. As man-made intelligence keeps on assuming a rising part in our lives, finding some kind of harmony between mechanical progression and moral responsibility is fundamental.

In the domain of medical care, the legitimate and moral contemplations are perplexing. Issues encompassing clinical protection, informed assent, and end-of-life choices have created broad legitimate systems and moral conversations. Regulations like the Health care coverage Versatility and Responsibility Act (HIPAA) safeguard patients' clinical data, while moral contemplations underscore regarding patients' independence and guaranteeing their prosperity.

One more huge area of lawful and moral concern is licensed innovation. Protected innovation regulations defend the manifestations of people and associations, empowering advancement and imagination. Moral contemplations in licensed innovation include finding some kind of harmony between safeguarding makers' freedoms and guaranteeing that information and culture stay available and open to all.

In contemporary society, a worldwide pandemic like the Coronavirus emergency has highlighted the significance of lawful and moral contemplations in general wellbeing. State run administrations have carried out measures to alleviate the spread of the infection, like lockdowns and obligatory inoculations. These actions, while planned to safeguard general wellbeing, likewise bring up issues about individual privileges and opportunities.

Moral contemplations in general wellbeing crises require finding some kind of harmony between individual freedoms and the aggregate prosperity. This includes straightforward correspondence, regard for independence, and guaranteeing that the actions taken are proportionate to the general wellbeing danger.

All in all, legitimate and moral contemplations are inseparably connected to the texture of contemporary society. Whether it's with regards to information security, natural manageability, civil rights, artificial intelligence, medical care, protected innovation, or general wellbeing, these contemplations shape our regulations, guide our way of behaving, and impact our shared mindset. As our reality keeps on advancing, it is urgent to stay cautious in maintaining and adjusting these legitimate and moral standards to address the difficulties and chances of the cutting edge age.

Chapter 4
Creating
Engaging
Content

In the advanced age, quality written substance is the final deciding factor, and commitment is the crown gem. Whether you're a blogger, online entertainment powerhouse, advertiser, or an entrepreneur, the capacity to make content that dazzles your crowd is fundamental. Drawing in satisfaction draws in and holds watchers as well as drives significant communications and transformations. In this complete aide, we will investigate the standards and methodologies for making content that gets and keeps up with the consideration of your crowd.

Figuring out Your Crowd

The most vital phase in making drawing satisfied is gripping your crowd. Without an unmistakable comprehension of who you're attempting to come to, fitting your substance to their necessities and interests is testing. Here are a few key contemplations:

Demographics: Know the age, orientation, area, and other segment data of your ideal interest group. This information assists you with making content that impacts them.

Psychographics: Grasp the qualities, convictions, interests, and way of life of your crowd. This information permits you to make content that lines up with their inclinations.

Difficulties and Problem areas: Recognize the issues and difficulties your crowd faces. Resolving these issues in your substance can be exceptionally captivating and significant.

Content Inclinations: Decide the sort of satisfied your crowd likes - articles, recordings, infographics, webcasts, and so on. Taking care of their inclinations increases commitment.

Narrating Matters

Individuals are normally attracted to stories. Stories are drawn in light of the fact that they summon feelings, make data more engaging, and make an association between the narrator and the crowd. This is the way to utilize narrating in your substance:

Close to home Allure: Make stories that summon feelings. Whether it's an inspiring tale or a grasping story, feelings make content significant.

Relatability: Share individual encounters and stories. Interesting stories make you more agreeable and genuine to your crowd.

Struggle and Goal: An exemplary narrating component is struggle trailed by goal. Present an issue and afterward give an answer inside your substance.

Use Visuals: Supplement your accounts with visuals. Pictures, recordings, and infographics improve the narrating experience.

Higher standards without ever compromising

It's enticing to produce content consistently, however quality ought to constantly outweigh amount. Bad quality substance may at first draw some consideration, however it won't keep your crowd locked in. Think about these angles:

Research: Concentrate on investigating your themes completely. Well-informed content is more educational and sound.

Originality: Be special and unique in your substance. Try not to just repeat what others have said. Offer a new point of view or remarkable experiences.

Clear and Succinct: Keep your substance clear and brief. Keep away from pointless language or filler text. A very much organized piece is simpler to follow.

Value: Continuously focus on offering some incentive to your crowd. Answer their inquiries, offer arrangements, and offer helpful data.

Charming Titles

The primary thing your crowd sees is the title. An enthralling title can have the effect between somebody tapping on your substance or looking past. Here are a few methods for making eye catching titles:

Be Unmistakable: Your title ought to give an unmistakable thought of what's going on with your substance. Keep away from misleading content strategies that can harm your believability.

Use Numbers: Mathematical records or measurements in titles can make your substance seriously engaging.

Trigger Feelings: Summon interest, humor, or some other feeling pertinent to your substance in the title.

Catchphrase

Improvement: Remember applicable watchwords for your titles for Web optimization purposes.

Visual Substance

Visuals are a useful asset for commitment. Whether it's pictures, recordings, infographics, or even GIFs, visual substance can essentially improve your message. This is the way to successfully utilize visuals:

Great Pictures: Utilize high-goal pictures that are pertinent to your substance. Low quality visuals can take away from the general nature of your substance.

Videos: Video content is exceptionally captivating. It tends to be utilized for instructional exercises, shows, narrating, and then some.

Infographics: Complex data can be rearranged and made more captivating through infographics.

Consistency: Keep a predictable visual style across your substance. This assists in working with marking acknowledgment.

Intuitiveness and Client Commitment

Empowering client cooperation can be a strong method for making your substance locking in. Here are a few techniques to accomplish this:

Remarks and Conversations: Energize remarks and conversations on your blog entries or virtual entertainment content. Answer remarks to cultivate commitment.

Surveys and Overviews: Use surveys and reviews to include your crowd and assemble their perspectives.

Tests and Challenges: Arrange tests or challenges connected with your substance. These can be fun and exceptionally captivating.

Clarify some things: Suggest conversation starters inside your substance to animate idea and collaboration.

Consistency is Critical

Consistency in your substance timetable and quality is fundamental. Your crowd ought to know what's in store from you. Consistency assembles trust and makes your crowd want more and more. Here are a few parts of consistency:

Content Schedule: Plan your substance ahead of time and adhere to a posting plan. This could be everyday, week by week, or whatever suits your crowd and limit.

Brand Voice: Keep a steady brand voice in your substance. This incorporates the tone, style, and informing.

Visual Marking: Utilize reliable marking components in visuals and designs, for example, logos, variety plans, and textual styles.

Investigation and Emphasis

To make the most captivating substance, you should investigate your presentation and make changes on a case by case basis. Watch out for measurements, for example, commitment rates, navigate rates, and offers. This is the way to actually repeat:

Audit Investigation: Routinely survey your substance examination to comprehend what's working and so forth.

A/B Testing: Explore different avenues regarding different substance types, titles, visuals, and presenting times to see what reverberates with your crowd.

Feedback: Pay attention to criticism from your crowd and make enhancements appropriately.

Outfitting the Force of Web optimization

Site improvement (Web optimization) is basic for content perceivability. To make your substance seriously captivating, it should initially be discoverable. Here are some Web optimization tips:

Watchword Exploration: Direct careful catchphrase examination to track down the most applicable and high-traffic watchwords in your specialty.

On-Page Website design enhancement: Enhance your substance for web search tools by remembering catchphrases for titles, headers, and all through the substance.

Meta Labels: Compose convincing meta titles and portrayals to increment navigate rates from web crawler results pages.

Portable Streamlining

In a time where most satisfaction is consumed on cell phones, upgrading your substance for versatility is basic.

This is the way to actually make it happen:

Responsive Plan: Guarantee your site and content are intended to adjust to different screen sizes and goals.

Quick Stacking Times: Portable clients have little tolerance for slow-stacking content. Upgrade your pictures and limit pointless contents.

Simple Route: Make it simple for portable clients to explore your substance. Utilize clear headings, buttons, and natural menus.

Building People group

Making a feeling of the local area around your substance can exceptionally lock in. This is the way to encourage this:

Virtual Entertainment Gatherings: Make or partake in web-based entertainment bunches connected with your specialty. These can be a center point for conversations around your substance.

Pamphlet Memberships: Urge your crowd to buy into your bulletin. This permits you to keep an immediate line of correspondence with your most drawn in supporters.

Live round table Discussions: Have live interactive discussions on stages like Facebook Live, Instagram Live, or YouTube. This continuous collaboration constructs a more grounded bond with your crowd.

Online Discussions: Partake in web-based gatherings and conversation sheets connected with your specialty. Share your ability and draw in with possible adherents.

Collaborations: Work together with other substance makers or powerhouses in your specialty. Cross-advancement can acquaint your substance with a more extensive crowd.

Validness and Straightforwardness

Crowds value validness and straightforwardness. Being veritable in your substance assists work with trusting and association. This is the way to integrate realness:

Honesty: Tell the truth and straightforward in your substance. Concede botches when they occur and share your excursion and encounters.

Behind-the-Scenes: Show in the background parts of your work or life. This gives your crowd a brief look into your genuine character.

Client Created Content: Urge your crowd to share their encounters or manifestations connected with your substance. Sharing client produced content shows the genuine effect of your work.

Individual Stories: Share individual stories and encounters that are pertinent to your substance. This refines your image and encourages a more profound association.

Profound Allure

Content that takes advantage of feelings will in general be seriously captivating. This is the way to add close to home allure for your substance:

Empathy: Comprehend the trouble spots and wants of your crowd and show compassion in your substance.

Moving Substance: Share accounts of achievement and motivation. Spur your crowd to make a move or conquer snags.

Uplifting tones: Make content that transmits inspiration and good faith. Energy is infectious and attracts individuals.

Utilization of Visuals: Emotive visuals, for example, pictures of individuals' appearances communicating different feelings, can make your substance all the more genuinely full.

Pattern Significance

Keeping your substance pertinent to latest things and occasions can support commitment. This is the way to consolidate trends

Content Planning and Production

An Essential Pair for Computerized Achievement

In the consistently developing computerized scene, content preparation and creation have become basic parts of any effective promoting procedure. The time of essentially producing content is a distant memory; presently, a smart and vital methodology is important to catch and hold a group of people's consideration. This article dives into the significance of content preparation and creation, investigates key procedures, and offers bits of knowledge on the most proficient method to tackle their power for greatest effect.

Grasping Substance Arranging

Content arranging is the groundwork of a fruitful substance promoting system. It includes an exhaustive evaluation of your interest group, objectives, and the stages where you mean to distribute your substance. Here are some fundamental viewpoints to think about:

Crowd Exploration: Your substance ought to resonate with your interest group. To do this, it's pivotal to comprehend their necessities, inclinations, trouble spots, and ways of behaving. Leading statistical surveying, making purchaser personas, and breaking down information are fundamental stages in this cycle.

Characterizing Objectives: What is it that you need to accomplish with your substance? Whether it's rising image mindfulness, driving site traffic, or producing leads, having distinct objectives will direct your substance creation and dissemination systems.

Content Schedule: A substance schedule is the guide for your substance creation. It helps you plan and arrange your substance endeavors, guaranteeing consistency and significance. A very much organized content schedule likewise empowers you to facilitate with your group and keep a consistent distributing plan.

Catchphrase Exploration: For Website design enhancement (Site improvement) objects, distinguishing significant catchphrases and expressions that your crowd is looking for is significant. Coordinating these into your substance can assist with working on your perceivability in web search tool results.

Dominating Substance Creation

Whenever you've illustrated a substance plan, now is the ideal time to execute it with accuracy. Content creation is where inventiveness, skill, and innovation merge to make convincing and connecting with materials. Here are a few methodologies to consider:

Great Substance: The bedrock of content creation is the production of superior grade, significant substance. Whether it's blog entries, recordings, webcasts, or infographics, the substance ought to be well-informed, elegantly composed, and outwardly engaging.

Variety of Configurations: Enhance your substance arrangements to take special care of various crowd inclinations. Recordings, for example, can catch the consideration of the people who lean toward visual substance, while articles or sites can draw in perusers who look for top to bottom data.

Consistency: Keeping up with consistency in your substance is crucial. It assembles trust and dependability with your crowd. Guarantee your substance lines up with your image, voice and values.

Enhancement for Website optimization: Consolidate on-page and off-page Website design enhancement methods. This incorporates utilizing applicable watchwords, advancing meta labels, and building backlinks to further develop web crawler rankings.

Dissemination System: Having first class happy isn't sufficient; it is necessary to arrive at your interest group. Utilize different dispersion channels, for example, web-based entertainment, email showcasing, and content partnership, to guarantee your substance contacts the perfect individuals.

The Advantageous Relationship

Content preparation and creation are innately interconnected. A thoroughly examined content arrangement sets the heading and targets for your substance creation endeavors. Consequently, happy creation impacts and refines the substance plan in view of what works best. This cooperative relationship is critical for a dynamic and versatile substance promoting procedure.

Advantages of an Agreeable Team

Effectiveness: Content arranging smoothes out the substance creation process. Understanding what should be made, when, and for whom decreases mystery and recovers time.

Further developed Pertinence: Content arranging guarantees that your substance lines up with your crowd's advantages and needs, bringing about additional significance and drawing in materials.

Consistency: With a substance schedule set up, you can keep a steady distributing plan, which is fundamental for holding your crowd's consideration.

Estimation and Variation: Content arranging assists you with setting KPIs (Key Execution Markers) that you can follow and examine. In view of the outcomes, you can adjust your substance creation systems for improved results.

Key Difficulties in Satisfied Arranging and Creation

Regardless of their significance, content preparation and creation accompany their portion of difficulties. Several typical examples include the following:

Content Over-burden: The advanced world is soaked with content. Standing apart from the group requires special, great substance.

Asset Requirements: Successful substance creation frequently requests time, ability, and instruments. Restricted assets can be an obstruction to creating outstanding substance.

Evolving Calculations: Web search tool calculations and online entertainment stages are continually developing. Remaining refreshed and adjusting your methodologies as needs be is critical.

Estimating return for capital invested: Evaluating the profit from ventures for content showcasing efforts can be challenging. Notwithstanding, with legitimate following and examination, you can acquire experiences into the presentation of your substance.

In the computerized age, content preparation and creation are not simply undertakings to mark off a rundown; they are basic drivers of online achievement. By putting time and exertion into figuring out your crowd, defining clear objectives, and making excellent substance, you can make a strong substance promoting system. This methodology, when executed with accuracy, can separate you from the opposition, draw in your crowd, and drive unmistakable outcomes. Keep in mind, content preparation and creation are not independent cycles; they are accomplices in a dynamic, continuous cycle that, when done well, yields significant prizes.

Authenticity and Trustworthiness

Genuineness and dependability are two crucial characteristics that shape our connections, whether individual or expert. In a world set apart by a computerized time of triviality and secrecy, these qualities have become progressively uncommon and, therefore, more significant. we will dig into the significant meaning of credibility and dependability, their transaction, and the effect they have on human association and cultural respectability.

Authenticity: The Embodiment of Self

Realness is a characteristic that mirrors the pith of one's actual self. It suggests genuineness, straightforwardness, and a readiness to be defenseless. Being genuine means remaining consistent with your convictions, values, and feelings, in any event, when confronted with cultural constraints or the compulsion to adjust. It's tied in with embracing your uniqueness and never undermining your respectability.

With regards to individual connections, legitimacy resembles the paste that ties individuals together. At the point when we experience credible people, we sense a profound association with them. Validness encourages trust since it permits others to perceive the truth about us. It empowers us to assemble authentic connections in light of common comprehension and regard.

Trustworthiness: The Structure Block of Trust

Reliability, then again, is an urgent component of any relationship. It includes reliably exhibiting dependability, respectability, and a pledge to staying faithful to one's commitments. At the point when we trust somebody, we accept that they will act to our greatest advantage, which creates a feeling of safety and profound association.

Validity and reliability are firmly interwoven. A valid individual is bound to be relied upon in light of the fact that their receptiveness and straightforwardness signal that they don't have anything to stow away. Alternatively, dependability supports credibility since it guarantees others that they can act naturally unafraid of judgment or treachery.

The Disintegration of Confidence in the Computerized Age

In the present advanced age, the ideas of credibility and dependability face novel difficulties. The web gives a stage to individuals to introduce cautiously organized forms of themselves, frequently darkening their actual personalities. Virtual entertainment, specifically, is known for cultivating a culture of approval chasing and triviality. This advanced scene can disintegrate trust since it's difficult to recognize validness and cunning. Individuals are much of the time uncertain whether the web-based persona introduced to them matches the genuine person of a person. Subsequently, we become more wary and reluctant to shape certified associations.

The Significance of Genuine Administration

In the expert world, legitimacy is essential for administration. Valid pioneers are open, fair, and veritable in their cooperations with representatives and partners. They won't hesitate to concede botches, share their qualities, and defend what they trust in. Such pioneers rouse trust and dependability among their colleagues.

Valid initiative likewise includes consistency. Pioneers who are legitimate in their qualities and activities construct trust since they can be depended upon to go with moral choices and completely finish their responsibilities. Interestingly, pioneers who need legitimacy frequently battle to acquire the trust and regard of their group.

In the public eye, the role of confidence

Trust isn't restricted to individual connections or authority; it is the foundation of a working society. Without trust, cultural designs separate. Trust empowers us to coordinate, exchange, and take part in an aggregate exertion for a long term benefit.

Lately, we have seen the outcomes of dissolving trust in organizations and in the public eye overall. At the point when trust is lost, it gives way to division, criticism, and social distress. Revamping trust requires a re-visitation of the standards of validness and dependability.

Encouraging Legitimacy and Dependability

Developing genuineness and dependability is an individual excursion. It starts with mindfulness and self-acknowledgement. Realness arises when people are in contact with their own qualities and are unafraid to communicate them. It likewise includes embracing weakness, which can be tested however is fundamental for building real associations.

Dependability, then again, relies on consistency and trustworthiness. To be viewed as dependable, one should respect responsibilities, be honest, and act in manners that line up with their expressed qualities. Dependability is certainly not a quality that can be faked; it should be shown through activities over the long run.

The Getting through Worth of Validness and Dependability

In reality as we know it where triviality and double dealing are progressively predominant, genuineness and dependability stay immortal excellencies. They are the mainstays of human association, whether in private connections, proficient settings, or inside the structure holding the system together.

To fabricate significant associations and encourage an additional dependable world, we should each endeavor to exemplify legitimacy and reliability. Thus, we can reinforce connections, sustain compelling authority, and add to the general prosperity of our networks. In a world starved for earnestness, these characteristics are the money of trust and the underpinning of a more associated and agreeable society.

Measuring the Impact of Content

The last decisive element in today's technological world is good written content.From blog entries and virtual entertainment updates to recordings and webcasts, content has turned into a foundation of showcasing and correspondence systems for organizations, people, and associations. Be that as it may, making content is only one piece of the situation; understanding and estimating the effect of that content is similarly fundamental. Estimating the effect of content is essential for surveying its adequacy, upgrading techniques, and accomplishing wanted objectives. In this article, we'll investigate the significance of estimating content effect and different strategies and measurements for doing as such.

The Meaning of Estimating Content Effect

Prior to plunging into the techniques for estimating content effect, it's fundamental to comprehend the reason why it's so significant. Content showcasing includes a critical venture of time and assets, and it's vital to realize whether it's yielding the ideal outcomes. Here are a few key motivations behind why estimating content effect is critical:

a. Evaluating Adequacy: Estimating content effect permits you to assess whether your substance is accomplishing its planned objectives. Is it safe to say that you are expanding brand mindfulness, producing leads, or driving deals? These inquiries can be addressed by breaking down satisfied influences.

b. Refining Procedures: By following the exhibition of your substance, you can distinguish what's working and what isn't. This information gives bits of knowledge to refine your substance promoting technique, advance substance, and improve future missions.

c. return for capital invested Assessment: Content showcasing frequently addresses a critical piece of a promoting spending plan. Estimating influence helps in deciding the profit from venture (return for money invested) and supporting the portion of assets to content creation.

d. Crowd Getting it: Content effect measurements can likewise uncover significant bits of knowledge about your crowd's inclinations, ways of behaving, and commitment levels. This information can illuminate future substance creation and focusing on.

Strategies for Estimating Content Effect

Estimating the effect of content includes a mix of quantitative and subjective strategies. The accompanying techniques and measurements can assist you with acquiring a thorough perspective on how your substance is performing:

a. Site Examination: Apparatuses like Google Examination give inside and out experiences into how guests associate with your substance. You can follow measurements, for example, site hits, skip rates, time on page, and transformation rates to evaluate the effect of your web content.

b. Web-based Entertainment Measurements: Virtual entertainment stages offer investigation that can assist with estimating the effect of your substance. You can follow commitment measurements like preferences, offers, remarks, and snaps. Also, checking devotee development can be a mark of content execution.

c. Email Promoting Measurements: For email content, open rates, navigate rates, and change rates are key measurements to quantify influence. These measurements give bits of knowledge into how well your email content is resounding with your crowd.

d. Website design enhancement Measurements: Website improvement (Web optimization) devices can assist with estimating how your substance positions in web search tool results pages. Higher rankings can prompt expanded natural traffic and are demonstrative of viable substance.

e. Change Following: Change following devices, for example, Google Label Supervisor, assist with estimating the effect of content concerning lead age and deals. You can credit changes to explicit substance pieces and comprehend their commitment to the general showcasing pipe.

f. Crowd Input: Subjective information from overviews, remarks, and direct criticism from your crowd can be important in evaluating content effect. These bits of knowledge give a more profound comprehension of what your substance is seen and its meaning for your crowd.

Key Substance Effect Measurements

To gauge content effect successfully, it's fundamental to center around unambiguous measurements that line up with your objectives. Here are a key substance influence measurements to consider:

a. Commitment Measurements: These measurements check how well your crowd is communicating with your substance and incorporate preferences, offers, remarks, and snaps. High commitment shows content reverberation.

b. Change Measurements: These measurements measure the capacity of your substance to change over perusers or watchers into leads or clients. Transformation rate, lead age, and deals are urgent in evaluating content effect.

c. Traffic Measurements: Traffic measurements uncover how successfully your substance is driving guests to your site. Site hits, remarkable guests, and reference sources can assist with surveying content effect.

d. Website design enhancement Measurements: Screen your substance's web index rankings, navigate rates (CTR), and natural traffic. Enhancements here demonstrate the substance's effect on search perceivability.

e. Time on Page: This measurement shows how long guests are spending on a particular piece of content. Longer normal time on a page can connote connecting with an important substance.

f. Social Sharing: The times your substance is shared via web-based entertainment stages are areas of strength for any of its effect and reach.

91

Setting Clear Goals

Prior to estimating the effect of your substance, setting clear objectives is significant.What do you hope to achieve with your substance? Could it be said that you are planning to increment brand mindfulness, produce leads, support deals, or instruct your crowd? By characterizing explicit objectives, you can tailor your substance and measurements to line up with your goals, making it more straightforward to successfully quantify influence.

Constant Observing and Enhancement

Estimating content effect is a continuous cycle. Content execution can change over the long haul, and it's fundamental to persistently screen measurements, distinguish patterns, and settle on information driven choices. Content enhancement ought to be a standard practice, directed by the experiences acquired from estimating influence.

Taking everything into account, estimating the effect of content is a fundamental part of any fruitful substance advertising methodology. It gives the bits of knowledge expected to survey viability, refine methodologies, and accomplish promoting objectives. By utilizing the different strategies and measurements examined in this article and setting clear goals, organizations and people can upgrade their substance endeavors and remain ahead in the serious computerized scene.

Chapter 5
Measuring Success and ROI

In the always developing scene of business and innovation, estimating achievement and profit from speculation (return on initial capital investment) has turned into an essential practice. No matter what the business or area, understanding the viability of one's endeavors and speculations is urgent for settling on informed choices and guaranteeing supportable development. In this exposition, we will investigate the idea of estimating achievement and return for money invested, the strategies and devices accessible for this reason, and the meaning of this training in the advanced business world.

Estimating achievement and return for money invested includes evaluating the results and productivity of different drives and speculations. This assessment cycle is crucial for organizations, not-for-profits, and even people endeavoring to accomplish their objectives. It gives an unmistakable comprehension of the worth produced by a specific venture, mission, or speculation and helps in settling on information driven choices.

To gauge achievement and return on initial capital investment really, one must initially characterize what achievement implies with regards to the particular undertaking. Achievement can take on different structures, from monetary benefits to expanded brand mindfulness, consumer loyalty, or social effect. Hence, setting clear and quantifiable goals is the underpinning of this interaction. Without clear cut objectives, it becomes testing to evaluate whether the results legitimize the speculations made.

When the objectives are laid out, the subsequent stage is to choose the fitting measurements and key execution pointers (KPIs) that line up with these goals. For monetary achievement, normal KPIs might incorporate income development, net revenues, and cost proficiency. Conversely, a charitable association zeroed in on friendly effect could utilize measurements like the quantity of lives improved, the personal satisfaction, or the decrease in a specific issue or issue.

In the domain of computerized showcasing, estimating achievement and return for money invested is a complex yet fundamental practice. Web based publicizing efforts, for example, depend vigorously on information examination to decide their adequacy. Measurements like navigate rates (CTR), change rates, and cost per obtaining (CPA) are imperative for figuring out the return on initial capital investment of web based advertising endeavors.

Moreover, web examination devices like Google Investigation offer exhaustive experiences into site traffic and client conduct, supporting advertisers in pursuing informed choices.

The accessibility of enormous information and progressed examination devices has reformed the manner in which organizations measure achievement and return for money invested. By gathering and breaking down immense measures of information, associations gain further experiences into their activities. AI and man-made reasoning (artificial intelligence) further upgrade these capacities, empowering prescient investigation and information driven direction. For example, proposal calculations utilized by online business stages increment deals as well as measure accomplishment through higher consumer loyalty and maintenance.

Notwithstanding computerized showcasing, the idea of estimating achievement and return on initial capital investment reaches out to different parts of current business, including item advancement, HR, and client support. For item advancement, associations frequently use measurements, for example, the net advertiser score (NPS) and consumer loyalty reviews to check the progress of their contributions. Representative turnover rates, worker commitment reviews, and execution measurements are regular in the domain of HR. In client assistance, reaction times, goal rates, and client criticism are fundamental signs of accomplishment and return on initial capital investment. While organizations are acquainted with estimating return on initial capital investment in monetary terms, taking into account the elusive parts of success is similarly significant. Consumer loyalty, brand notoriety, and worker confidence can fundamentally affect long haul achievement, regardless of whether their impact is trying to evaluate. For example, an organization that puts resources into worker preparation and improvement may not quickly see a direct monetary return, however after some time, this speculation can prompt a more gifted and persuaded labor force, adding to better progress over the long haul.

The techniques and instruments for estimating achievement and return on initial capital investment keep on developing to stay up with the powerful business climate. Among these, the reasonable scorecard approach is generally utilized. It assesses accomplishment through four viewpoints: monetary, client, inward cycles, and learning and development. By taking into account numerous parts of the business, the reasonable scorecard gives a more comprehensive perspective on exhibition and return on initial capital investment.

Profit from venture is in many cases determined utilizing a direct equation: return on initial capital investment = (Net Benefit/Cost of Speculation) x 100. Be that as it may, this recipe can be adjusted to different settings. For instance, in computerized promotion, return for money invested may be determined as (Income Created - Advertising Expenses)/Showcasing Expenses. In a not-for-profit setting, return for capital invested can be evaluated by contrasting the expense of running projects with the social effect accomplished.

Aside from these techniques, devices like client relationship the executives (CRM) frameworks, venture asset arranging (ERP) programming, and task board programming assume a vital part in estimating achievement and return for capital invested. These frameworks help associations track and investigate information connected with their activities, clients, and undertakings, working with the appraisal of execution and monetary results.

The meaning of estimating achievement and return for money invested in the cutting edge business world couldn't possibly be more significant. It guides associations in upgrading their procedures, speculations, and asset designation. Also, it assists in distinguishing regions that require improvement and regions where achievement can be scaled. Organizations that disregard to quantify achievement and return for capital invested risk settling on ignorant choices and passing up amazing learning experiences.

The act of estimating achievement and return for money invested is especially significant with regards to maintainability and corporate social obligation (CSR). Many organizations are perceiving the significance of natural and social obligation, and they are integrating these standards into their business procedures. Estimating the outcome of these drives frequently includes evaluating their ecological effect, like diminished fossil fuel byproducts or expanded utilization of sustainable power, and their social effect, including working on working circumstances or backing for neighborhood networks.

Besides, financial backers and partners are progressively intrigued by organizations' natural, social, and administration (ESG) execution. Estimating and revealing ESG measurements has turned into a standard practice for organizations looking to draw in capable financial backers and show their obligation to moral and feasible strategic policies. The outcome of ESG drives is evaluated through different measurements, including ESG appraisals and supportability reports.

All in all, estimating achievement and return for capital invested is a basic practice in the present business scene. It permits associations to assess the results of their endeavors, speculations, and drives, whether they are monetary, functional, or social in nature. Setting clear goals, choosing proper measurements, and utilizing progressed devices and examination are fundamental stages in this cycle. The capacity to quantify achievement and return on initial capital investment enables organizations to go with informed choices, adjust to evolving conditions, and flourish in an undeniably aggressive and socially cognizant world. While the techniques and devices for estimation keep on advancing, the center rule stays consistent: understanding the worth created by one's activities is the way to economical achievement.

Key Performance Indicators (KPIs)

In the present quick moving and cutthroat business climate, achievement is much of the time estimated by the capacity to adjust, improve, and accomplish targets. Key Execution Pointers (KPIs) assume a vital part in this pursuit. KPIs are quantifiable measurements that assist associations with assessing their presentation, settle on informed choices, and eventually drive achievement. We dig into the universe of KPIs, analyzing their importance, types, execution, and the more extensive effect they have on organizations.

Characterizing KPIs:

At its center, a KPI is a mathematical worth that shows how really an organization is accomplishing its vital and functional objectives. KPIs give a reasonable and quantifiable perspective on an organization's advancement towards its targets. They act as a compass for direction, guaranteeing that associations stay on the right course and make essential changes when deviations happen.

The Meaning of KPIs:

KPIs are not simply numbers; they are the soul of viable administration. They offer a few benefits:

Clarity: KPIs improve on complex execution information into a couple of key figures, pursuing it simpler for choice creators to handle and follow up on.

Accountability: By setting and following KPIs, organizations lay out responsibility among groups and people. At the point when explicit KPIs are not met, clear necessities to make a move.

Focus: KPIs guarantee that assets are diverted toward the most basic regions. Organizations can recognize what is working and what needs improvement.

Measurement: KPIs give a standard to constant improvement. They offer a place of correlation with survey the viability of procedures and drives.

Kinds of KPIs:

KPIs can be sorted into a few kinds in view of their motivation and application:

Monetary KPIs: These pointers survey the monetary wellbeing and execution of an association. Models incorporate income development, overall revenue, and profit from speculation.

Functional KPIs: These KPIs center around functional proficiency and viability. Measurements like process duration, quality, and asset use fall into this classification.

Client KPIs: Estimating consumer loyalty, degrees of consistency, and Net Advertiser Score (NPS) assists associations with understanding how well they are serving their clients.

Worker KPIs: These KPIs check representative execution and commitment, including measurements like worker turnover, efficiency, and fulfillment.

Deals and Showcasing KPIs: Organizations use KPIs, for example, change rates, lead age, and client securing cost to screen deals and advertising endeavors.

Project The board KPIs: Project-related KPIs assist with following undertaking progress, cutoff times, and financial plan adherence.

Executing KPIs:

To execute KPIs successfully, an organized methodology is essential:

Characterize Clear Targets: Begin by laying out clear, reachable targets. KPIs ought to be lined up with these targets.

Select the Right KPIs: Pick KPIs that straightforwardly influence your objectives. Try not to set such a large number of KPIs, as this can weaken concentration and viability.

Gather Information: Assemble exact and dependable information. This might require putting resources into information assortment devices and frameworks.

Set Targets: Characterize explicit targets or benchmarks for each KPI. These ought to be aggressive yet sensible.

Track and Investigate: Routinely screen and dissect KPIs. Dashboards and announcing instruments can improve on this interaction.

Follow up on Results: At the point when KPIs show deviations from targets, make a suitable move. This might include process enhancements, asset assignment, or key movements.

Audit and Adjust: Occasionally survey the pertinence of your KPIs. As business conditions change, KPIs might be acclimated to reflect new needs.

The More extensive Effect of KPIs:

KPIs expand their impact past individual organizations. They add to monetary development, intensity, and the general nature of items and administrations:

Financial Development: By empowering organizations to zero in on proficiency and adequacy, KPIs add to financial development. Further developed execution and benefit lead to expanded venture and occupation creation.

Competitiveness: Organizations that effectively use KPIs will generally be more cutthroat in their enterprises. These organizations stay receptive to advertise elements, client needs, and arising patterns.

Quality Improvement: KPIs are frequently attached to quality control measures. Organizations that focus on KPIs are bound to give greater items and administrations.

Development and Variation: In a quickly impacting world, flexibility is vital. KPIs assist organizations with recognizing when systems need change, encouraging development and flexibility.

Asset Productivity: KPIs drive asset productivity. By intently observing asset usage, associations diminish squander and further develop maintainability.

All in all, Key Presentation Markers are not simply numbers on a calculation sheet. They are useful assets that guide organizations towards progress. When nicely picked and actually carried out, KPIs explain goals, cultivate responsibility, and drive execution upgrades. They come in different sorts to suit various regions of an association and act as an impetus for monetary development, seriousness, and quality improvement. KPIs have become fundamental instruments for current business the board, empowering associations to explore the intricacies of a unique world and arise as victors in their separate fields.

Analyzing Engagement and Conversions

In the advanced age, organizations endeavor to bridle the force of the web to reach and connect with their main interest group. Whether you're a web based business store, a substance driven site, or a specialist co-op, understanding the elements of commitment and transformations is critical to your prosperity. We will dig into the complexities of investigating commitment and transformations, taking apart what they mean, how to quantify them, and why they are basic for business development.

Engagement: The Heartbeat of Association

Commitment addresses the cooperation between your crowd and your computerized stage, be it a site, web-based entertainment profile, or versatile application. It fills in as a gauge for the viability of your substance and client experience. Commitment can appear in different structures, including likes, remarks, shares, navigate rates, and time spent on a site page. Understanding these collaborations assists you with fitting your substance and plan to all the more likely resound with your crowd.

Estimating commitment frequently begins with quantitative measurements, like the quantity of preferences, offers, and remarks. Nonetheless, this information just starts to expose what's underneath. Subjective commitment, which incorporates opinion examination and client input, is similarly imperative. It can give bits of knowledge into the feelings and inclinations of your crowd, permitting you to make content that reverberates on a more profound level.

Conversions: Transforming Commitment right into it

While commitment addresses the underlying interest, transformations are the sacred goal. A transformation is the ideal move you maintain that your crowd should initiate, be it making a buy, pursuing a pamphlet, or mentioning a statement. The change rate is a basic measurement for evaluating the viability of your computerized showcasing endeavors.

Change rate is determined as the quantity of transformations separated by the absolute number of guests or commitment. For instance, on the off chance that 1,000 individuals visit your internet business site, and 50 of them make a purchase, your transformation rate is 5%. This measurement assists you with checking the effectiveness of your computerized channel and recognizing regions that might require enhancement.

Examining Commitment to Upgrade Changes

Commitment and transformations are complicatedly connected. An elevated degree of commitment frequently connects with an improved probability of changes. At the point when your crowd is effectively partaking with your substance or stage, they are more disposed to make the following stride, which might be making a buy or finishing up a contact structure.

Breaking down commitment information can offer significant bits of knowledge into how to improve your transformation rate. For example, you might find that blog entries with longer normal perusing times are bound to prompt item page visits. Equipped with this data, you can make a greater amount of the substance that keeps clients drawn in and draws them nearer to change.

The Significance of A/B Testing

A/B testing is a key strategy for dissecting commitment and improving transformations. It includes making two renditions of a site page, email, or ad, with one variable changed. By parting your crowd and showing each gathering one of the two renditions, you can figure out which variation is more viable concerning commitment and change.

For instance, if you need to expand the active clicking factor of your email crusade, you could A/B test two headlines. By following open rates and navigate rates for each title, you can figure out which one reverberates better with your crowd. This iterative cycle permits you to ceaselessly refine your procedures.

The Job of Information Examination
Information examination devices assume a vital part in the examination of commitment and changes. They assist organizations with gathering, process, and decipher huge volumes of information to extricate significant experiences. For instance, Google Examination offers a plenty of measurements, including skip rate, meeting length, and change following, which can support understanding how clients collaborate with your site.

Besides, AI and man-made reasoning have entered the field, giving prescient investigation. These calculations can gauge client conduct and prescribe customized content to improve commitment and improve the probability of changes.

The Force of Retargeting
Few out of every odd guest will change over on their most memorable visit. This is where retargeting becomes possibly the most important factor. By following client conduct and serving fitted promotions or content to the people who have recently drawn in with your foundation, you can urge them to return and finish the ideal activity.

Retargeting uses commitment information to make a more customized client experience. This works on the possibilities of change as well as sustains client reliability. The more somebody interfaces with your image, the more certain they are to trust your items or administrations.

Taking everything into account

Breaking down commitment and transformations is a complex undertaking that consolidates quantitative and subjective information, testing techniques, information examination, and customized procedures. These viewpoints exchange to give an exhaustive comprehension of client conduct and how to improve your computerized presence for business development.

Eventually, commitment and changes are advantageous. An elevated degree of commitment fills in as the pathway to transformations, while changes give the unmistakable outcomes that characterize your business' prosperity. By ceaselessly examining and refining your way to deal with commitment and transformations, you can remain ahead in the advanced scene and meet the developing requirements of your crowd.

Calculating Return on Investment (ROI)

Profit from Speculation (return for money invested) is a central monetary metric that surveys the productivity of a venture or a business. It is an urgent device for independent direction, permitting people and associations to assess the proficiency and viability of their ventures. Return on initial capital investment is communicated as a rate and gives significant bits of knowledge into the expected increases or misfortunes related to a specific venture. In this article, we will dive into the idea of return for money invested, its importance, and how to really work it out.

Grasping return for money invested

Return on initial capital investment is a presentation measure that assists people and organizations with assessing the return created from a particular venture contrasted with its expense. Generally, it evaluates the advantage acquired comparable to the underlying capital cost. Return on initial capital investment is especially significant in pursuing informed monetary choices, whether it relates to individual speculations, business activities, or advertising efforts.

Meaning of return for capital invested

The meaning of return for capital invested can be featured by its application in different situations:

Venture Choices

Return for capital invested assumes a significant part in deciding the feasibility of likely speculations. Financial backers frequently utilize this measurement to look at changed venture valuable open doors. By evaluating the normal return on initial capital investment, they can go with informed decisions in regards to where to assign their assets.

Business Execution

For organizations, return on initial capital investment is a critical mark of execution. It helps in evaluating the progress of different drives, from sending off new items to extending tasks. Business pioneers can advance asset allotment by examining the return for money invested in various undertakings.

Showcasing and Publicizing

In showcasing and publicizing, return on initial capital investment is a basic device for assessing the viability of missions. Organizations can survey which promoting channels or methodologies yield the best returns, empowering them to distribute their showcasing spending plans all the more proficiently.

Cost Decrease

Return for money invested can likewise be utilized to assess cost decrease drives. At the point when organizations carry out cost-cutting measures, they can compute the return on initial capital investment of these progressions to guarantee they are financially savvy and economical over the long haul.

Risk Evaluation

Understanding return on initial capital investment is fundamental for assessing risk. By evaluating the likely return against the underlying speculation, financial backers and organizations can decide if an endeavor merits going after. A high return for capital invested may show a high-risk venture, while a lower return for money invested could suggest a more steady and open door.

Ascertaining return on initial capital investment

return on initial capital investment is a clear yet strong metric that can be determined utilizing the accompanying equation:

makefile

Duplicate code

return on initial capital investment = (Net Benefit/Introductory Speculation) * 100

To ascertain return on initial capital investment really, understanding the parts of this formula is fundamental:

Net Benefit

Net benefit addresses the income produced from the speculation short of all expenses related to it. This incorporates costs like working expenses, charges, and some other applicable consumptions.

Introductory Venture

The underlying speculation is the aggregate sum of capital put resources into the undertaking or resource. It includes the buy cost as well as any extra costs like upkeep, remodel, or arrangement costs.

Deciphering the Outcomes

Whenever you've determined return for capital invested utilizing the equation, you will get a rate. This rate shows the profit from speculation. A positive return for money invested infers that the venture produced a benefit, while a negative return for money invested proposes a misfortune. The bigger the return for money invested, the more beneficial the venture.

Illustration of return for money invested Estimation

To outline the idea of return on initial capital investment, we should think about a speculative interest in a stock:

Introductory Venture: $10,000

Net Benefit Following One Year: $2,000

Utilizing the return on initial capital investment equation:

slam

110

Duplicate code
return for money invested =
($2,000/$10,000) * 100 = 20%
In this model, the return for money invested is 20%, and that implies that the interest in the stock yielded a 20% return in one year. This rate can be utilized to contrast the presentation of this venture and other possible open doors.

Restrictions of return for capital invested While return on initial capital investment is an important measurement, it has a few restrictions:

Time span

Return for capital invested estimations are in many cases in light of a particular time span, like one year. This can prompt varieties in results, and the decision of time span ought to be painstakingly thought of.

Disregards Chance

Return for money invested doesn't represent the degree of chance related to a venture. A high return for capital invested doesn't guarantee that speculation is generally safe, and a low return on initial capital investment isn't guaranteed to demonstrate a high-risk venture.

Doesn't Consider Opportunity Cost

Return on initial capital investment just thinks about the profit from the particular speculation and doesn't consider the possible returns from elective ventures.

Profit from Speculation (return for capital invested) is a fundamental monetary metric that guides in assessing the productivity and proficiency of ventures. Whether for individual monetary choices, business undertakings, or showcasing systems, return for money invested gives significant experiences into the possible returns or misfortunes.

Understanding the parts of return for money invested and how to ascertain it is fundamental for settling on informed monetary choices. While return for money invested is a significant device, it ought to be utilized related to other monetary measurements to acquire an exhaustive comprehension of a venture's true capacity.

Chapter 6 Emerging Trends in Influencer Marketing

Lately, force to be reckoned with promoting has developed from a specialty technique to a standard publicizing channel. Brands across the globe are focusing on teaming up with virtual entertainment powerhouses to arrive at their ideal interest groups. The scene of force to be reckoned with advertising is dynamic, continually moving as it adjusts to changes in shopper conduct, innovation, and online entertainment stages. In this article, we will investigate the absolute most conspicuous arising patterns in powerhouse showcasing.

Miniature and Nano Powerhouses: While large scale forces to be reckoned with and superstars have been the focal point of powerhouse showcasing, there's a developing movement towards miniature and nano forces to be reckoned with. These people might have more modest followings, yet they frequently have exceptionally connected with and faithful crowds. Working with miniature and nano powerhouses can be financially savvy and result in additional true associations with purchasers.

Legitimacy and Straightforwardness: As powerhouse promoting has developed, so has the crowd's interest for credibility and straightforwardness. There's a developing pattern of powerhouses sharing their genuine lives, battles, and real conclusions. This shift is driven by purchasers' longing for trustworthiness and credibility in the substance they draw in with.

Long haul Associations: Brands are progressively creating some distance from the present moment, value-based associations with powerhouses. Long haul organizations are turning out to be more normal, permitting forces to be reckoned with to coordinate a brand into their substance profoundly. This gives a more certifiable and normal method for advancing items or administrations.

Various and Comprehensive Missions: Variety and incorporation are presently key contemplations for powerhouse showcasing efforts. Brands are perceiving the significance of working with powerhouses from different foundations, nationalities, sexual orientations, and capacities to contact a more assorted crowd.

Video Strength: Video quality written substance makes all the difference in the force to be reckoned with promoting the world. Stages like TikTok, Instagram Reels, and YouTube have acquired huge fame. Short-structure video content is especially compelling, and marks are benefiting from this pattern to connect with crowds.

Transient Substance: Stories on stages like Instagram and Snapchat have a need to get moving and FOMO (Anxiety toward Passing up a major opportunity) that catches crowds' consideration. Brands are utilizing transient substance through powerhouse associations to make a feeling of promptness and fervor around their items or advancements.

Client Created Content: Empowering powerhouses and supporters to create content connected with a brand has turned into a pattern. Client created content aides construct a local area around a brand and takes into consideration a more true and differed portrayal of the item.

Simulated intelligence and Information driven Choices: Man-made consciousness and information examination are assuming an undeniably critical part in force to be reckoned with promoting. Brands use simulated intelligence apparatuses to distinguish the most reasonable powerhouses for their missions and to successfully follow the exhibition of missions more.

Maintainability and Social Obligation: Powerhouses are turning out to be more vocal about friendly and natural issues. Brands are lining up with powerhouses who share their qualities and can advance their manageability drives, assisting with improving their standing.

Livestream Shopping: Livestream shopping is a pattern that has picked up speed, particularly in business sectors like China. Brands band together with powerhouses who host live shopping occasions, where watchers can straightforwardly buy items exhibited during the livestream.

Virtual Powerhouses: Virtual forces to be reckoned with, made utilizing CGI and trend setting innovation, are doing something significant. These computerized personas can be completely controlled and prearranged, furnishing brands with a remarkable method for drawing in with their crowd.

Specialty People group: Instead of zeroing in exclusively on the quantity of devotees, brands are searching for powerhouses who include serious areas of strength for an inside specialty networks. These powerhouses can significantly affect exceptionally specific objective business sectors.

Gamification: Integrating gamification components into force to be reckoned with showcasing efforts is turning out to be more normal. Brands use challenges, challenges, and intuitive encounters to connect with crowds and make a feeling of fun around their items.

Administrative Consistence: States and virtual entertainment stages are turning out to be more severe about powerhouse showcasing guidelines. Brands are zeroing in on following these guidelines to keep up with their standing and stay away from legitimate difficulties.

Virtual and Increased Reality: Virtual and expanded reality innovations are being utilized to make vivid powerhouse encounters. These innovations permit buyers to attempt items prior to pursuing a buy choice essentially.

All in all, force to be reckoned with promoting is a quickly developing field. The patterns referenced above mirror the changing scene of customer inclinations, innovation progressions, and the developing virtual entertainment stages. Brands that adjust to these arising patterns will be better situated to associate with their main interest groups and remain ahead in the consistently aggressive universe of powerhouse advertising. It's fundamental for advertisers to remain informed and be light-footed in their systems to saddle the maximum capacity of this powerful showcasing channel.

Live Streaming and Short-Form Video

In the speedy universe of advanced media, live real time and short-structure recordings have arisen as two strong and extraordinary apparatuses. They have re-imagined the manner in which we consume content, associate with our crowd, and even earn enough to pay the bills in the computerized age. This investigation dives into the elements of live web based and short-structure video, revealing insight into their importance, development, and the effect they have had on our lives.

Live Streaming: A Constant Association

Live streaming has reformed the manner in which we convey and share encounters. It empowers people and organizations to communicate video content progressively to a worldwide crowd. This immediate association significantly affects how we experience occasions, letting it be known, amusement, and even instruction. Live streaming offers a feeling of instantaneousness that customary media can't coordinate. Watchers can draw in with content as it unfurls, encouraging a feeling of being available at the occasion.

The ascent of live real time stages like Jerk, YouTube Live, and Facebook Live has permitted another age of content makers to arise. Gamers, artists, culinary experts, and, surprisingly, ordinary people can now share their gifts, interests, and day to day routines with a crowd. These stages have democratized content creation, making it open to anybody with a cell phone and a fantasy.

Experience streaming's intelligent nature is another key component. Watchers can leave remarks, seek clarification on some pressing issues, and even make money related commitments during communication. This continuous criticism circle supports a more grounded connection among makers and their crowd. Content makers can adjust on the fly, answering crowd responses and ideas, making a customized and dynamic experience.

Experience streaming's impact stretches out past amusement. It has turned into a significant instrument for organizations and associations. Organizations utilize live spilling for item dispatches, virtual meetings, and, surprisingly, in the background looks into their activities. It permits a worldwide crowd to associate with brands in manners that were beforehand impossible.

Short-Structure Video: Snackable and Shareable

Short-structure video, then again, addresses an alternate feature of our computerized media scene. Stages like TikTok, Instagram Reels, and Plant (before its suspension) have advocated the idea of scaled down satisfaction. Short-structure recordings commonly range from a couple of moments to several minutes, making them simple to consume and share.

The allure of short-structure video lies in its curtness. In reality as we know it where abilities to focus are diminishing, these recordings are intended to catch interest inside the initial couple of moments. They can be entertaining, instructive, or sincerely full in a reduced configuration. This snackable substance is ideal for our in a hurry society.

The viral idea of short-structure recordings is striking. A very much created video can rapidly gather a large number of perspectives and sling its maker to moment popularity. TikTok, specifically, has made stars out of common people, displaying the democratizing force of virtual entertainment. The "For You Page" calculation on TikTok is intended to open clients to content customized to their inclinations, encouraging a feeling of personalization and keeping them locked in.

Besides, short-structure recordings have turned into a foundation of online entertainment promotion. Brands influence this configuration to make drawing in, shareable substance. It is a more open and savvy way for organizations to interface with more youthful crowds who are progressively disenthralled with customary promotion. The arrangement is especially successful for narrating and item showings.

The Intermingling: Live Web based and Short-Structure Video

Live web based and short-structure video are not fundamentally unrelated; they frequently coincide. Many substance makers utilize short-structure recordings to advance their live streams. They make secrets, features, and pieces of their live happy to draw in watchers and produce expectation.

Moreover, stages like Instagram Live and Facebook Live permit clients to save their live transmissions as recordings after the stream has finished. These recorded live recordings become a type of short-structure content, making a double reason approach that profits by the qualities of the two configurations.

Difficulties and Concerns

While live web based and short-structure video have achieved energizing changes in the advanced scene, they are not without their difficulties. Protection concerns, control of content, and copyright issues are continuous issues that stages and makers should address. The appeal of moment distinction can likewise have disadvantages, for example, cyberbullying and psychological well-being issues for makers.

Also, the calculations and curation practices of these stages bring up issues about protected, closed off environments and channel bubbles, where clients are simply presented to content that lines up with their current convictions and interests. This can restrict the variety of points of view clients experience, a question of critical cultural concern.

All in all, live web based and short-structure video have changed how we make, consume, and associate with advanced media. They offer ongoing associations and reduced down, shareable substance that take care of our quick moving lives. These arrangements have altered amusement, advertising, and correspondence, setting out new open doors and difficulties. As the advanced scene keeps on developing, live web based and short-structure video will without a doubt stay at the very front of this computerized insurgency.

The Rise of Niche Influencers

In the consistently developing scene of virtual entertainment and computerized showcasing, another type of powerhouses has arisen and acquired unmistakable quality as of late. These are the specialty forces to be reckoned with, people who have cut out a devoted continuing in unambiguous, frequently barely characterized areas of interest. While conventional powerhouses, with their large number of supporters, stay persuasive, specialty powerhouses are leaving their imprint by associating with exceptionally drew in crowds in remarkable and significant ways.

The Force of Specialty

Specialty powerhouses center around specific topics or interests, for example, veggie lover cooking, metropolitan planting, one of a kind style, or 3D printing. What separates them is the profundity of their insight and energy for their picked specialty. This mastery permits them to resonate with a profoundly designated crowd who share a similar energy. While they might not have a great many devotees, their more modest, more drawn in networks have gigantic incentive for brands and advertisers.

The Trust Variable

Specialty powerhouses frequently have a more significant degree of trust with their crowd. When a force to be reckoned with is seen as a specialist in their specialty, their suggestions convey huge weight. Supporters are bound to trust their judgment and be impacted by their substance since they accept that the powerhouse really thinks often about the specialty and isn't simply advancing items for benefit. This trust can prompt more compelling showcasing lobbies for brands.

Validness and Association

One of the critical qualities of specialty powerhouses is their validness. They're not advancing a wide exhibit of items; all things considered, they're centered around their specialty and the items and administrations that truly line up with it. This credibility causes their suggestions to feel more certified and less like an attempt to sell something. Their association with the specialty and their crowd is substantial, which is an important resource in the computerized promoting world.

Profoundly Drew in Crowds

Specialty powerhouses frequently have more modest but more drawn in followings. These adherents are energetic about the specialty, making them more open to the force to be reckoned with content and proposals. Commitment rates, like likes, remarks, and offers, are frequently higher for specialty powerhouses contrasted with their standard partners. This elevated degree of commitment implies that a brand's message can contact an exceptionally open crowd.

Cost-Adequacy

Working with specialty powerhouses can be more practical for brands. While large scale powerhouses with a great many devotees can order high expenses for advancements, specialty powerhouses frequently have more sensible valuing. This permits more modest organizations with restricted spending plans to take advantage of the force of powerhouse promoting. Also, the profit from speculation (return on initial capital investment) can be higher while working with specialty powerhouses, as the crowd is more designated and locked in.

Genuine Narrating

Specialty forces to be reckoned with succeed at valid narrating. They can wind around a story around an item or administration that feels certified and convincing. Their capacity to share individual encounters, tips, and counsel connected with the specialty makes areas of strength for a with their crowd. This narrating can be an important device for brands hoping to pass on their message in an engaging and sincerely thunderous manner.

Difficulties and Dangers

While specialty forces to be reckoned with offer various benefits, there are additional difficulties and dangers to consider. For example, the restricted size of their crowd implies that the range may be more modest contrasted with standard powerhouses. Brands ought to likewise cautiously vet specialty powerhouses to guarantee they line up with the brand's qualities and objectives. Moreover, the fast development of the powerhouse scene has raised worries about credibility and straightforwardness, as some specialty forces to be reckoned with may turn to exploitative practices to acquire adherents or supporters.

The Fate of Specialty Forces to be reckoned with

Specialty powerhouses are not a passing pattern; they address a crucial change in the powerhouse showcasing scene. As purchasers become seriously knowing and search out credible, specific substance, specialty powerhouses will keep on assuming an imperative part in molding computerized promoting procedures.

Brands that embrace this pattern and work together with specialty powerhouses can take advantage of exceptionally drawn in, designated crowds and make more significant associations with their clients.

All in all, the ascent of specialty forces to be reckoned with is a demonstration of the developing idea of computerized showcasing.

These powerhouses have demonstrated that a more modest, drawn in crowd can be as significant, while perhaps not all the more in this way, than a huge following.

Their legitimacy, skill, and capacity to interface with their specialty settle on them a convincing decision for brands hoping to make significant promoting efforts. As the powerhouse scene keeps on developing, specialty forces to be reckoned with will stay a main impetus in forming the future of powerhouse promoting

Influencer Marketing Automation

Powerhouse showcasing robotization is a strong technique that has gotten forward movement lately. This approach uses innovation and information to smooth out and improve the force to be reckoned with, making it more productive and successful. In this article, we will investigate the idea of a powerhouse promoting mechanization, its advantages, difficulties, and a few prescribed procedures.

Grasping Force to be reckoned with Promoting Mechanization

Powerhouse showcasing is a type of virtual entertainment advertising that includes teaming up with people who have a critical web based following to advance items, administrations, or brands. Customarily, this interaction included broad manual work, from distinguishing expected forces to be reckoned with to arranging contracts, following execution, and estimating return for capital invested.

Force to be reckoned with showcasing robotization, nonetheless, includes utilizing programming and instruments to rearrange and speed up these undertakings. The mechanization of powerhouse advertising incorporates different phases of the cycle, including force to be reckoned with revelation, relationship with the board, content creation, crusade execution, and execution examination.

The Advantages of Powerhouse Advertising Mechanization

Proficiency: Computerization lessens the time and exertion expected for powerhouse recognizable proof and effort. High level calculations can investigate huge measures of information to track down the most reasonable powerhouses for a specific brand or mission.

Scalability: Robotization permits brands to at the same time work with various powerhouses. This implies missions can contact a bigger and more different crowd, which is fundamental for organizations intending to extend their market reach.

Targeting: Robotization devices can section forces to be reckoned with in light of their specialty, crowd socioeconomics, and commitment levels. This accuracy in focusing on guarantees that brands team up with powerhouses who can successfully contact their ideal crowd.

Information   Driven Choices: Mechanization devices give ongoing investigation, empowering brands to quantify the progress of their powerhouse crusades precisely. This information driven approach considers fast changes and improvements during a mission.

Consistency: Mechanization guarantees that powerhouse promoting efforts follow a predictable system, message, and timetable. This can assist with building up a brand's personality and message across different powerhouses' foundations.

Challenges in Force to be reckoned with Showcasing Mechanization

While powerhouse advertising computerization offers various advantages, it isn't without its difficulties. Here are a few normal obstacles that brands might confront:

Validness   Concerns: The computerized idea of powerhouse promoting can now and again think twice about legitimacy of the substance. It's fundamental for brands to track down a harmony among mechanization and keep up with the real voice of the powerhouse.

Calculation   Restrictions: While calculations are strong, they are not faultless. Brands ought to in any case practice human judgment in powerhouse determination and mission technique to stay away from unanticipated entanglements.

Oversaturation: As additional brands go to powerhouse promoting, there's a gamble of oversaturation on the lookout.

This can prompt crowd exhaustion and diminished commitment. Brands should be key and inventive to stick out.

Powerhouse

Connections: Robotization can in some cases depersonalize force to be reckoned with connections. Keeping areas of strength for a powerhouses is critical for effective, long haul coordinated efforts.

Best Practices in Force to be reckoned with Promoting Computerization

To take advantage of powerhouse showcasing robotization, think about the accompanying prescribed procedures:

Clear Goals: Characterize your objectives and KPIs (Key Execution Pointers) prior to beginning any mission. This guarantees that your mechanization endeavors line up with your general advertising methodology.

Better standards without compromise: Try not to focus on the quantity of forces to be reckoned with over the nature of their substance and crowd commitment. Select powerhouses that truly resound with your image.

Crowd Exploration: Completely comprehend your main interest group to choose powerhouses who can associate with them actually.

Legitimate Consistence: Guarantee that your powerhouse organizations follow important guidelines and rules, like exposure necessities and protection regulations.

Steady Observing: While computerization can smooth out many assignments, standard checking is fundamental. Watch out for crusade execution, powerhouse content, and crowd criticism.

Flexibility: Be available to changes and turns during a mission. Robotization devices can give information to assist you with settling on informed choices continuously.

Powerhouse showcasing mechanization has changed the manner in which brands draw in with their ideal interest group through virtual entertainment. By utilizing innovation and information, organizations can distinguish, work together with, and measure the effect of powerhouses all the more actually. While difficulties and entanglements exist, a very much arranged robotization technique, combined with best practices, can result in fruitful powerhouse promoting efforts that drive brand development and commitment. As the scene of computerized advertising keeps on developing, force to be reckoned with promoting computerization is ready to assume a considerably more huge part in the business.

Chapter 7
Case Studies and Success Stories of Real-

World Examples of Effective Influencer Campaigns

As of late, powerhouse showcasing has arisen as a strong system for brands to interface with their interest group. It uses the ubiquity and genuineness of people who have fabricated an unwavering following via web-based entertainment, empowering brands to advance items or administrations in a more engaging and connected way. To delineate the capability of powerhouse crusades, we should dig into a couple of contextual investigations and examples of overcoming adversity of certifiable models that have accomplished exceptional outcomes.

Daniel Wellington: An Immortal Story of Progress

Daniel Wellington, a Swedish watch organization, executed one of the most notable powerhouse promoting efforts. They teamed up with an extensive variety of miniature powerhouses, essentially on Instagram. These forces to be reckoned with shared top notch photographs of themselves wearing Daniel Wellington watches, exhibiting the item's tastefulness and effortlessness. The mission's prosperity is ascribed to the durable taste of the powerhouse posts and the brand's moderate personality. Within a couple of years, the brand's income soared from a little startup to a worldwide peculiarity, producing more than $200 million in income in 2016.

Level Belly Tea: Changing Wellbeing with Powerhouses

Level Belly Tea changed the wellness and health industry with their detox tea item. They worked with powerhouses, fundamentally wellness lovers and wellbeing advocates, who might post about their encounters with the tea. These forces to be reckoned with shared their stories, underlining the item's job in accomplishing a level stomach and further developed wellbeing. The mission's prosperity was obvious through the gigantic development in the brand's online entertainment following, with a huge expansion in deals, because of the powerhouses' appeal and declarations.

H&M: Breaking the Web with Powerhouse Supported Assortments

H&M, a worldwide style goliath, saddled the force of powerhouses to effectively send off its assortments. They teamed up with style powerhouses, VIPs, and fashioners, who made expectation and energy by posting sneak looks and wearing pieces from the forthcoming assortments. This methodology permitted H&M to make a buzz via online entertainment and produce long lines at their stores when the assortments were delivered. It's a perfect representation of how powerhouse showcasing can mix with customary retail techniques to incredible impact.

Airbnb: Building Trust with Host Stories

Airbnb, the web-based excursion rental stage, perceived that trust was a critical consideration for individuals booking facilities in another person's home. They started a mission where hosts imparted their own accounts and encounters to Airbnb. These accounts featured the glow and realness of Airbnb stays. The "Host Stories" crusade prevailed with regards to building trust and reinforcing the brand's association with the two hosts and visitors, at last helping appointments.

Glossier: Co-Creation with Powerhouses

Glossier, a wonder and skincare brand, participated in co-creation with powerhouses and clients to foster new items. They paid attention to client criticism and teamed up with powerhouses to comprehend what the market wanted. This straightforward methodology prompted the shipment of fruitful items like "Kid Forehead" and "Cloud Paint." By including their ideal interest group in the item improvement process, Glossier fabricated an energetic local area and accomplished noteworthy development.

Red Bull: Outrageous Games and Content Creation

Red Bull has reliably shown the force of content-driven powerhouse advertising. They support outrageous competitors and back them in making thrilling and frequently popular substances. This methodology has extended their image a long way past caffeinated drinks, partner Red Bull with experience and stretching the boundaries. Models incorporate Felix Baumgartner's supersonic drop from the edge of room and their sponsorship of different outrageous games.

All in all, these contextual analyses and examples of overcoming adversity embody the flexibility and effect of force to be reckoned with showcasing in the advanced business scene. By utilizing the believability and reach of powerhouses, brands have accomplished exceptional outcomes, from dramatic income development to making strong networks around their items or administrations. As the computerized scene keeps on developing, powerhouse showcasing is probably going to stay a critical driver of brand achievement, interfacing with purchasers on an individual and engaging level.

Lessons Learned from Influencer Marketing Pioneers

In the consistently developing scene of computerized promoting, powerhouse showcasing has arisen as a strong and dynamic device for brands to interface with their interest groups. Over the course of the last ten years, powerhouse showcasing has developed from a clever investigation to an extravagant industry, and the trailblazers of this field bring important examples to the table. As organizations and advertisers keep on exploring the universe of powerhouse showcasing, here are a few key examples gained from the individuals who prepared.

Credibility is Central

One of the most pivotal illustrations from force to be reckoned with promoting pioneers is the significance of legitimacy. Powerhouses who have gathered the most achievement are the individuals who keep up with their certifiable selves and are straightforward with their adherents. Crowds are attracted to validness; they can detect trickiness well in advance. At the point when powerhouses stay consistent with their personality and line up with brands that mirror their qualities, the message resounds all the more emphatically with their devotees. Inauthentic joint efforts can prompt a deficiency of validity for both the powerhouse and the brand.

Pick the Right Fit

Force to be reckoned with promoting is certainly not a one-size-fits-all procedure. Trailblazers in this field have reliably stressed the meaning of finding powerhouses who line up with the brand's qualities, interest group, and objectives. Fundamental to pick forces to be reckoned with have a veritable interest in the items or administrations they are advancing. A marvel powerhouse probably won't be the most ideal decision for a tech device, as well as the other way around. Trailblazers have shown that fruitful powerhouse showcasing efforts are based on the underpinning of major areas of strength for a pertinent fit between the force to be reckoned with and the brand.

Miniature Forces to be reckoned with Can Sneak up suddenly

While many partner powerhouse advertising with superstar supporters, trailblazers in the field have exhibited the effect of miniature forces to be reckoned with. These are people with more modest yet exceptionally drawn in followings inside a particular specialty. Miniature powerhouses frequently have a more private association with their supporters, prompting more significant levels of trust and commitment. Working with miniature powerhouses can be financially savvy and yield amazing outcomes, especially for brands focusing on specialty markets.

The decisive component is ultimately excellent written content.

Extraordinary substance is at the center of powerhouse advertising achievement. Forces to be reckoned with are content makers, and their capacity to create drawing in, applicable, and imaginative substance separates them. Illustrations from pioneers show that effective associations include cooperation between the brand and force to be reckoned with to make content that flawlessly incorporates the item or administration while offering some incentive to the crowd. Superior grade, outwardly engaging, and useful substance can enamor crowds and drive results.

Long haul Connections

Fabricating long haul associations with powerhouses is a significant illustration gained from force to be reckoned with showcasing pioneers. Rather than one-off crusades, brands benefit from progressing organizations with powerhouses who truly resound with their crowd. These connections advance into real supports and add to supported brand perceivability and trust. Trailblazers have demonstrated the way that sustaining such connections can prompt common development and achievement.

Information Driven Direction

In the beginning of force to be reckoned with advertising, it was trying to actually gauge return for capital invested. Nonetheless, trailblazers in the field have featured the significance of information driven navigation. Using examination and following devices to quantify commitment, reach, and transformations is presently standard practice. Brands can streamline their force to be reckoned with promoting endeavors by examining information to refine methodologies and augment their profit from speculation.

Consistence and Straightforwardness

The powerhouse advertising scene is advancing, and administrative bodies are turning out to be more watchful. Trailblazers have discovered that consistency and straightforwardness are non-debatable. Brands and powerhouses should comply with pertinent promoting rules and unveil paid organizations. This straightforwardness fabricates entrust with the crowd and shields against expected legitimate issues. It's fundamental for brands to teach powerhouses about these guidelines to keep up with moral practices.

Adjust to Changing Stages

Virtual entertainment stages and patterns are steadily changing, and trailblazers have taken in the worth of versatility. Fruitful powerhouse showcasing efforts include keeping awake to-date with the most recent stage elements, calculations, and crowd conduct. What dealt with Instagram a couple of years prior may not be as compelling today. Trailblazers constantly develop their techniques to stay applicable in an always moving computerized scene.

Be Ready for Analysis

Powerhouse advertising doesn't come without its reasonable portion of analysis. Trailblazers have discovered that few out of every odd mission will be generally welcomed, and there will continuously be cynics. It's fundamental for brands and powerhouses to be ready for both positive and negative input. Tending to analysis with beauty and transparency can transform naysayers into likely backers.

Enhance and Investigation

The trailblazers of force to be reckoned with promoting have reliably pushed the limits and embraced development. They comprehend that the business is dynamic and cutthroat. The illustrations gained from these trailblazers underline the significance of exploring different avenues regarding groundbreaking thoughts, stages, and configurations. Being available to develop and evaluate new methodologies can prompt noteworthy missions that catch the crowd's consideration.

All in all, powerhouse promoting has made some amazing progress since its commencement, and the examples gained from its trailblazers have formed the methodologies that we see today. Legitimacy, cautious force to be reckoned with determination, content quality, long haul connections, information driven choices, consistency, flexibility, versatility despite analysis, and a promise to development are key focus points from the trailblazers of powerhouse showcasing. As the business keeps on developing, these illustrations will stay important for brands and advertisers hoping to use the force of powerhouse promoting to interface with their interest groups.

Chapter 8
Challenges and Pitfalls Avoiding Common Mistakes in

Influencer Marketing

Force to be reckoned with promoting has turned into a pervasive procedure in the realm of computerized showcasing. Brands across different businesses have understood the capability of utilizing powerhouses to contact a more extensive crowd and lay out a more unique interaction with their objective market. Be that as it may, while powerhouse showcasing can be an integral asset, it isn't without its difficulties and entanglements. In this article, we will investigate a portion of the normal mix-ups made in force to be reckoned with showcasing and examine how to keep away from them.

Picking Some unacceptable Powerhouses:

One of the most well-known botches in powerhouse promoting is choosing forces to be reckoned with who are not ideal for your image. This frequently happens when brands focus on a force to be reckoned with compass or adherent count over their pertinence to the item or message. To stay away from this entanglement, it's crucial for research and recognize powerhouses whose qualities, interests, and crowd line up with your image.

Teaming up with powerhouses who really interface with your item will yield more true and successful showcasing efforts.

Overlooking Miniature Forces to be reckoned with:

While it's enticing to work with super powerhouses with a huge number of supporters, overlooking miniature powerhouses can be a critical mix-up. Miniature forces to be reckoned with frequently have exceptionally drawn in and steadfast adherents who trust their suggestions. They can give a more savvy choice for brands hoping to arrive at a particular specialty crowd. Try not to underrate the force of realness and trust that miniature powerhouses can bring to your mission.

Absence of Legitimacy:

Legitimacy is the foundation of force to be reckoned with promoting. In the event that your powerhouse's support of your item or administration feels constrained or undependable, it can harm your image's standing. Try not to prearrange powerhouses too vigorously and permit them to make content in their own voice and style. Crowds are bound to believe forces to be reckoned with who truly put stock in and utilize the items they advance.

Ignoring Straightforwardness:

Straightforwardness is critical in force to be reckoned with advertising. Both powerhouses and brands ought to plainly reveal their connections. Neglecting to do so can prompt legitimate issues and, all the more significantly, dissolve trust among the crowd. Guarantee that your powerhouse associations are set apart as supported or #ad, following significant publicizing guidelines.

Setting Unreasonable Assumptions:

Many brands expect moment results from force to be reckoned with promoting. While it can yield phenomenal return on initial capital investment, it's fundamental to comprehend that force to be reckoned with promoting is a drawn out system. Building brand mindfulness and trust takes time.

Try not to anticipate unexpected phenomena, and be ready to put resources into long haul organizations with powerhouses.

Sitting above Happy Quality:

The nature of the substance made by forces to be reckoned with can fundamentally influence the progress of a mission. A few brands tragically think twice about satisfied quality to save costs. Top notch content is fundamental for connecting with the crowd and establishing a long term connection. Put resources into proficient substance creation to guarantee your image is addressed well.

Not Estimating return for money invested:

Powerhouse showcasing efforts ought to be results-driven. A few brands fall into the snare of not estimating the profit from venture (return for money invested) really. Use the following instruments and measurements to evaluate the effect of your missions. Set clear targets and measure how force to be reckoned with associations add to accomplishing those objectives.

Conflicting Brand Informing:

It's fundamental to keep up with consistency in your image informing across all showcasing channels, including powerhouse coordinated efforts. Irregularities can confound the crowd and weaken your image character. Give powerhouses brand

140

rules to guarantee that your message is imparted successfully.

Disregarding the Drawn out Relationship:

Building an oddball organization with a powerhouse may not yield the best outcomes. Growing long haul associations with powerhouses can prompt more real and significant joint efforts. It permits powerhouses to turn out to be valid brand advocates, which resounds better with their crowd.

Disregarding the Legitimate Perspective:

Force to be reckoned with advertising is dependent upon different legitimate guidelines, including copyright and protected innovation regulations. Brands should guarantee that they have the important privileges to utilize content made by powerhouses and conform to appropriate regulations and guidelines in their promoting endeavors.

Unfortunate Correspondence:

Compelling correspondence is fundamental for a fruitful powerhouse showcasing effort. Absence of clear correspondence can prompt errors, missed cutoff times, and below average substance. Keep up with open and straightforward correspondence with your powerhouses to guarantee that everybody is in total agreement.

Overlooking Investigation and Criticism:

Marks frequently botch the chance to gain from their force to be reckoned with crusades by disregarding the investigation of information and criticism. Use investigation instruments to comprehend what's working and so forth, and be available to input from both forces to be reckoned with and the crowd. Utilize this data to refine and work on future missions.

All in all, powerhouse showcasing can be a strong device when executed accurately. To stay away from normal missteps and traps, brands ought to focus on credibility, straightforwardness, and a drawn out approach.

By picking the right forces to be reckoned with, encouraging certifiable connections, and keeping up with exclusive expectations in happy quality, brands can tackle the maximum capacity of powerhouse promoting while at the same time staying away from the entanglements that can impede its viability.

Keep in mind, powerhouse showcasing is a unique field, so keeping awake to-date with patterns and developing your systems is vital to progress.

Dealing with Controversies and Crisis Management

In the present speedy and interconnected world, debates and emergencies can strike any association, huge or little. How a business or element deals with these difficulties can represent the deciding moment of its standing and long haul achievement. Debates can go from item reviews to virtual entertainment stumbles, while emergencies could incorporate cataclysmic events, monetary embarrassments, or network protection breaks. No matter what the idea of the

142

episode, a powerful emergency the board is essential to explore these violent waters and arise more grounded on the opposite side.

One crucial guideline of emergency the board is to be ready. Organizations ought to have an emergency the executives plan set up before any issues emerge. This plan ought to include key leaders inside the association as well as specialists in advertising, lawful, and correspondence fields. By having a reasonable hierarchy of leadership and characterized jobs, an association can answer all the more quickly and proficiently.

The most vital phase in managing debates and emergencies is to recognize the issue. Straightforwardness is critical. Stowing away or making light of an issue can intensify what is going on and hurt an association's standing. Conceding the issue and showing a guarantee to tending to it is the most important move toward the goal.

Then, evaluating what is happening degree and impact is fundamental. Is it a disengaged episode or part of a bigger issue? Understanding the full degree of the emergency will illuminate direction. For example, assuming that an item has an imperfection that represents a gamble to purchasers, a review might be important. Conversely, a virtual entertainment debate could require an open acknowledgment and an adjustment of procedure.

Correspondence is a focal mainstay of emergency the board. It is imperative to speak with inside and outside partners speedily and truly. Workers ought to be educated regarding what is going on and any actions they ought to take. Outside interchanges ought to be created cautiously, conveying compassion and obligation. Web-based entertainment and official statements can be incredible assets, however they should be utilized reasonably and honestly.

Online entertainment can be both a gift and a revile in emergency the board. On one hand, it permits associations to rapidly contact a tremendous crowd. Then again, it can intensify contentions and give a stage to pundits. Overseeing online entertainment successfully implies tending to worries and reactions deferentially and speedily. Disregarding or taking part in web-based contentions can hurt an association's picture. It's likewise essential to remain cautious and screen web-based entertainment for arising issues.

At times, it might very well be important to include an emergency the executives master or advertising firm. These experts can offer direction on correspondence techniques and assist with exploring the perplexing scene of general assessment. They can likewise give important bits of knowledge into dealing with the story and relieving reputational harm.

Lawful contemplations ought not be ignored. Contingent upon the idea of the emergency, there might be administrative or lawful ramifications. It's fundamental to talk with lawful specialists to guarantee consistency and relieve any expected legitimate dangers. Tending to legitimate worries close by correspondence endeavors can assist an association with keeping up with believability and trust.

As an association manages an emergency, it ought to zero in on correcting the issue and forestalling future events. This might include interior examinations, item reviews, process upgrades, or changes in corporate culture. Showing a pledge to gaining from the emergency and forestalling its repeat can assist with remaking entrust with partners.

Debates and emergencies frequently accompany a monetary effect. Loss of income, lawful costs, and harm to the brand can all influence an association's primary concern. Monetary arranging ought to be a piece of emergency for the board, including saving stores for such occasions and surveying the drawn out monetary effect.

It's vital to perceive that an emergency can make enduring impacts. Indeed, even after the quick issue is settled, an association might keep on confronting reputational challenges. Long haul endeavors to reconstruct trust and exhibit obligation to positive change are fundamental. Organizations like Johnson and Johnson, after the Tylenol emergency, have had the option to recapture the trust of their clients through a supported obligation to somewhere safe and straightforwardness.

One vital part of emergency the board is gaining from the experience. After an emergency, an association ought to lead a post-emergency survey. What worked out in a good way? What might have been done another way? What examples can be applied to future circumstances? This growing experience can prompt better emergency the executives systems and more prominent strength even with future difficulties.

All in all, managing debates and emergencies the board is a fundamental expertise for associations in the cutting edge world. Being ready, straightforward, and informative are essential standards. By recognizing issues, evaluating their effect, and taking quick, fitting activity, an association can explore emergencies all the more really. Including specialists in advertising, lawful, and emergency the executives can give important direction. Through cautious correspondence, lawful contemplations, and a pledge to tending to the base of the issue, an association can modify trust and arise more grounded from an emergency. Ultimately, the significance of gaining from the experience and utilizing those illustrations to further develop emergencies the board ought to be considered carefully. In this present reality where contentions and emergencies are unavoidable, powerful emergencies the executives is a basic part of progress.

Chapter 9
The Future of
Influencer

Marketing Predictions and Speculations

Lately, powerhouse promoting has arisen as a strong and groundbreaking power in the realm of publicizing and marketing. Online entertainment stages have turned into the new fields for powerhouse joint effort, and as we plan ahead, we can expect a few vital patterns and improvements that will shape the business.

Miniature Forces to be reckoned with Will Overwhelm: The period of super powerhouses with a great many supporters is moving towards miniature forces to be reckoned with. These people have more modest yet profoundly drawn in devotee bases, making their suggestions more genuine and significant. Brands will progressively zero in on organizations with miniature powerhouses who are seen as more dependable.

Credibility Will Be Principal: Crowds are turning out to be really knowing, requesting validness from forces to be reckoned with. Thus, we can expect a shift away from excessively prearranged and cleaned content towards additional genuine and engaging posts. Validness will be the key part of fruitful powerhouse advertising efforts.

Video Content Will Win: The ascent of stages like TikTok and the precedence of YouTube highlight the rising significance of video content. Brands will collaborate with powerhouses to make drawing in and engaging video content to associate with their crowds.

Specialty Powerhouses Will Flourish: The one-size-fits-all approach will give way to specialty powerhouses who take care of exceptionally unambiguous crowds. Brands will investigate these specialties to really arrive at their optimal customers more.

Long haul Organizations: Brands will put resources into long haul associations with powerhouses instead of oddball crusades. This approach can fabricate more grounded associations with powerhouses and their crowds and lead to additional steady and feasible outcomes.

Virtual and Expanded Reality: As innovation propels, we can expect the rise of virtual forces to be reckoned with, symbols, and AR encounters. These computerized personas will give new chances to brands to associate with crowds in novel and vivid ways.

Information Driven Navigation: The future of powerhouse advertising will be progressively information driven. Brands will depend on cutting edge investigation to quantify the progress of missions, figure out crowd conduct, and select the most reasonable powerhouses for their items or administrations.

Administrative Changes: As powerhouse advertising develops, we can expect stricter guidelines to guarantee straightforwardness and buyer security. Powerhouses and brands should adjust to new rules and divulgence necessities.

Eco-Accommodating Force to be reckoned with

Promoting: Supportability and eco-cognizance will turn out to be more conspicuous in force to be reckoned with showcasing. Brands will collaborate with powerhouses who line up with their ecological qualities and work on, mirroring the more extensive shift towards manageability.

Livestream Shopping: Live Streaming, which has acquired prominence in business sectors like China, will probably turn out to be more normal in force to be reckoned with promoting. Watchers can look for items while watching powerhouses, giving a consistent shopping experience.

Artificial intelligence Controlled Content: Man-made consciousness will assume a critical part in force to be reckoned with showcasing. Man-made intelligence can assist powerhouses and brands with distinguishing patterns, upgrade content, and anticipate crowd conduct, prompting more successful missions.

Client Created Content: Brands will urge their clients to make content, a growing powerhouse promoting to regular buyers. Client created content can upgrade brand realness and cultivate local area commitment.

Intuitive Substance: Forces to be reckoned with and brands will make more intuitive substance, like surveys, tests, and difficulties, to draw in crowds and drive cooperation.

Worldwide Reach: As stages and markets keep on globalizing, powerhouse showcasing will reach out to worldwide crowds. Powerhouses from various districts will team up with brands to arrive at a more extensive client base.

Ascent of simulated intelligence Powerhouses: While virtual powerhouses have previously done something worth remembering, the man-made intelligence controlled powerhouses representing things to come could be vague from people, offering new and special open doors for promotion.

All in all, powerhouse promotion is developing at a quick speed. The future will be portrayed by credibility, miniature powerhouses, video content, and information driven independent direction. The business will keep on adjusting to new advancements and administrative changes while investigating imaginative ways of connecting with crowds and assemble enduring brand-buyer connections. As we look forward, these forecasts and hypotheses are probably going to shape the unique scene of force to be reckoned with.

How Technology and Consumer Behavior May Shape the Future

Innovation and buyer conduct are two dynamic and interwoven powers that have been forming the present and will without a doubt keep on embellishing what's in store. As we stand at the slope of another time, it's urgent to look at how these elements will combine and drive changes in different ventures and parts of our lives.

Not long ago, the connection among innovation and buyer conduct was generally uneven. Advancements in innovation directed how buyers communicated with the world. The presentation of the web, for instance, upset how individuals got to data, shopped, and conveyed. This shift constrained buyers to adjust and embrace these freshly discovered abilities.

Today, in any case, the connection among innovation and shopper conduct is undeniably more advantageous. Shoppers use extensive impact, forming the course and speed of innovative headways. This developing relationship is supposed to significantly affect what's in store.

One of the key regions where innovation and buyer conduct will converge is in the domain of personalization. Shoppers have generally expected customized encounters in their communications with innovation. From Netflix suggesting films in light of your review history to Amazon proposing items, personalization has turned into the standard. This pattern will just heighten in the future as artificial intelligence and AI become significantly more refined. Purchasers will come to expect administrations and items custom fitted to their remarkable inclinations and requirements.

The impact of shopper conduct should be visible in the developing interest for practical and eco-accommodating items. As shoppers become more aware of their ecological effect, innovation organizations are answering with inventive arrangements. Electric vehicles, environmentally friendly power sources, and brilliant home frameworks are instances of how innovation is lining up with the upsides of buyers. Later on, this pattern is supposed to speed up, with shoppers driving the turn of events and reception of green innovations.

The computerized change of enterprises will keep on being a predominant subject from here on out. The Coronavirus pandemic sped up the reception of remote work, telemedicine, and online business, showing that the digitalization of different areas isn't just imaginable however frequently more effective. This adjustment of shopper conduct will push organizations to put resources into innovation to fulfill the advancing needs of their clients. The ascent of computer generated reality and expanded reality will additionally upset enterprises like instruction, medical care, and amusement, offering vivid encounters that line up with changing shopper inclinations.

Besides, the ascent of the Web of Things (IoT) will assume an urgent part coming soon for innovation and shopper conduct. IoT gadgets are turning out to be progressively incorporated into our regular routines, from savvy indoor regulators that conform to our inclinations to wearable wellness trackers that screen our wellbeing. These gadgets give important information, which organizations can use to comprehend and anticipate buyer conduct. Protection and information security will be principal worries in this time, as purchasers wrestle with the compromise among accommodation and shielding their own data.

The manner in which we shop is going through a huge change, and this is obvious in the fast development of online business. Web based shopping is advantageous and frequently more practical than customary physical retail. Shoppers value the capacity to think about items, read surveys, and make buys from the solace of their homes. Innovation assumes a critical part in upgrading the web based business experience through highlights like virtual attempts and expanded reality item shows. Later on, we can anticipate that web based business should develop, with headways in strategies and conveyance techniques, including drone conveyances and computerized distribution centers.

One more entrancing part representing things to come is the changing scene of transportation. The improvement of independent vehicles is set to change the manner in which individuals drive and transport merchandise. Self-driving vehicles can possibly improve security, decrease gridlock, and give versatility answers for the people who can't drive. Notwithstanding, this shift will likewise challenge laid out ventures, for example, collision protection and ride-sharing. Purchaser conduct will shape the reception of independent vehicles, as confidence in the innovation, guidelines, and individual inclinations will all assume critical parts in deciding how rapidly this change happens.

The medical services industry is likewise on the cusp of significant changes. Telemedicine and advanced wellbeing stages have become progressively famous, offering patients the comfort of virtual conferences and remote observing. The Coronavirus pandemic sped up the reception of these innovations, and buyer conduct has moved to acknowledge far off medical care as a practical choice. Accordingly, the medical services industry is probably going to keep putting resources into innovation to work on understanding consideration and smooth out processes.

Taking everything into account, what's to come is obviously impacted by the intermingling of innovation and shopper conduct. Personalization, supportability, computerized change, the Web of Things, online business, transportation, and medical services are only a couple of regions where these two powers will shape the scene. It's a demonstration of the consistently advancing nature of our general public, where purchasers are not just uninvolved beneficiaries of innovation but rather dynamic members in its turn of events and application. As we explore the intricacies of this unique relationship, one thing is sure: the future will be set apart by an entrancing interaction between the requests and wants of purchasers and the imaginative capacities of innovation.

CONCLUSION

The Ongoing Importance of Influencer Marketing

All in all, force to be reckoned with promoting keeps on being a fundamental and consistently developing part of present day showcasing methodologies. Throughout the long term, it has changed the manner in which brands draw in with their crowds and advance their items or administrations. This getting through significance can be ascribed to a few key variables, which I will dive into in this closing conversation.

One of the essential explanations behind the continuous meaning of force to be reckoned with promoting is its capacity to lay out realness and validity. As purchasers are barraged with customary notices and attempts to sell something, they have become progressively adroit at sifting through inauthentic messages. Powerhouses, then again, are viewed as confided in voices inside their specialties. Their crowds have a veritable association with them, frequently thinking of them as companions or specialists in their particular fields. When a powerhouse advances an item or administration, it conveys a degree of legitimacy and trust that is difficult to accomplish through traditional publicizing strategies.

Additionally, powerhouse promoting has adjusted to the changing elements of advanced media. In the period of promotion blockers and the decay of customary publicizing channels, force to be reckoned with advertising has prospered. It is a type of publicizing that flawlessly incorporates into the substance purchasers are as of now consuming. Powerhouses produce content that is drawing in and applicable, making it not so much meddling but rather more interesting to their crowds. This flexibility to changing purchaser propensities has helped force to be reckoned with showcasing keep up with its significance in the always developing scene of advanced promoting.

The continuous significance of powerhouse promoting can likewise be credited to its capacity to contact exceptionally designated crowds. Powerhouses frequently have a profound comprehension of their devotees, knowing their socioeconomics, interests, and inclinations. This information permits brands to miniature objective their missions and contact the right crowd with the right message. In this present reality where one-size-fits-all promoting procedures are turning out to be less viable, powerhouse showcasing gives a strong answer for arriving at specialty markets.

Notwithstanding the capacity to contact explicit crowds, powerhouse showcasing is financially savvy. While customary promoting strategies can be restrictively costly, teaming up with powerhouses frequently gives a better yield on venture. Powerhouse showcasing efforts are in many cases more reasonable and offer a more straightforward line to possible clients. The expenses of delivering content are much of the time divided among the brand and the powerhouse, making it a more financial plan accommodating choice, particularly for little and medium-sized organizations.

Besides, powerhouse showcasing is a flexible device in a brand's promoting stockpile. It very well may be utilized for different purposes, from raising brand attention to sending off new items or administrations. It can likewise be utilized for building long haul brand associations or for transient special missions. This flexibility permits organizations to tailor their powerhouse advertising procedures to their particular objectives, whether that is driving deals, expanding memorability, or just captivating with their crowd.

The continuous significance of powerhouse showcasing is additionally intently attached to the social verification it gives. In reality as we know it where online surveys and companion suggestions vigorously impact buying choices, force to be reckoned with supports go about as a type of social confirmation. When a force to be reckoned with advances an item, their devotees are bound to see it decidedly and think of it as worth difficult. This social approval can essentially influence buyer conduct, cultivating a feeling of trust and validity around a brand or item. One more vital angle is the capacity of powerhouse showcasing to produce client created content. At the point when forces to be reckoned with make content around a brand's item or administration, it frequently motivates their devotees to do likewise. This client created content not just fills in as free promoting for the brand yet in addition gives an additional bona fide and engaging point of view, as it comes straightforwardly from fulfilled clients. This pattern of content creation can intensify the compass and effect of a force to be reckoned with advertising effort.

Powerhouse promoting isn't without its difficulties and concerns, nonetheless. As the business has developed, issues connected with straightforwardness, realness, and moral contemplations have arisen. Fundamental for brands to work with powerhouses line up with their qualities and message, and to guarantee that supported substance is plainly named thusly. Besides, the continually changing calculations via virtual entertainment stages can make it trying to keep up with reliable reach and commitment, which requires a degree of spryness and versatility with respect to both powerhouses and brands.

All in all, powerhouse promoting has shown to be something other than a passing pattern in the realm of computerized showcasing. Its continuous significance is attached in its capacity to lay out genuineness and believability, adjust to changing media elements, contact exceptionally designated crowds, remain financially savvy, and proposition flexibility for different showcasing goals. Moreover, the social evidence and client created content it produces keep on driving its importance in the present advertising scene.

While difficulties and concerns remain, powerhouse promoting's persevering through significance is a demonstration of its viability in a world immersed with publicizing messages. Brands that influence powerhouse showcasing shrewdly and morally stand to profit from its ability to draw in, convince, and make enduring associations with customers in a computerized age where genuineness and trust are central.

www.ingramcontent.com/pod-product-compliance
Lightning Source LLC
Chambersburg PA
CBHW072205290526
45794CB00004B/1654